CANE, RUSH AND *willow*

CANE, RUSH AND *willow*

Weaving with natural materials

HILARY BURNS

FIREFLY BOOKS

A FIREFLY BOOK

First published in Canada in 1998 by
Firefly Books Ltd.
3680 Victoria Park Avenue
Willowdale, Ontario, Canada
M2H 3K1

Published in the United States in 1998 by
Firefly Books (U.S.) Inc.
P.O. Box 1338, Ellicott Station
Buffalo, New York, USA
14205

Cataloguing in Publication Data

Burns, Hilary
Cane, rush, and willow: weaving with natural materials

Includes index.
ISBN 1-55209-260-7

1. Handweaving. 2. Fiberwork. I. Title

TT873.E87 1998   746.41   C97-932764-4

This book was designed and produced by
Quintet Publishing Limited
6 Blundell Street, London N7 9BH

Creative Director: Richard Dewing
Art Director: Clare Reynolds
Design: Lucy Parissi and Caroline Grimshaw
Project Editor: Doreen Palamartschuk
Photographer: John Melville
Illustrator: Valerie Hill

Typeset in Great Britain by Central Southern Typesetters, Eastbourne
Manufactured in Singapore by United Graphic Pte Ltd
Printed in China by Leefung-Asco Pte Ltd

The publishers acknowledge the financial support of the Government of Canada through the
Book Publishing Industry Development Program for our publishing activities.

PUBLISHER'S NOTE

Working with the tools and materials in this book can be dangerous. Always exercise extreme caution
and follow the instructions carefully and the safety procedures recommended. As far as the methods
and techniques mentioned in this book are concerned, every effort has been made to ensure that all
information is accurate. However, conditions, tools, and individual skills vary.
Neither the author, copyright holder, nor the publisher can be responsible for any injuries,
losses, or other damages which may result from the use of the information in this book
or can accept any legal liability for errors or omissions.

ACKNOWLEDGMENTS

I would like to thank the following people who have helped me become a basketmaker or in the
production of this book. And that means all the contributors who have given so much of their time,
energy, and expertise; and the people who have shared with me their love of materials and techniques,
and taught me so much. Among many are Mary Butcher, Lois Walpole, Joe Hogan, Colin Manthorpe, and
Hisako Sekijima, also Mick Jones, who taught me how to make hurdles. My thanks go to Sook
Shackleton for her support and help, to Inez Heath for asking the "why" questions, to Bonnie Gale for
answering my queries about North America, and to all the students who have made me think about the
way things are done. To Sean Hellman, who made the ash and chestnut stools on pages 92, 95 and 97.
To Mike Ingram of the National Trust, Kingswear, Devon in the UK, for providing a lake and transport for
the coracle launch. Above all, thanks go to my family, David, Emma, Olivia, and Jerome for living with all
the "sticks and twigs" that are part of basketmaking. Last, but not least, I thank John Melville for his
patience with the photography and Diana Steedman for asking me to write this book.

Contents

Introduction

In writing this book I have aimed to show how a wide range of textile and basketmaking techniques can be used in a creative way. Any one of these techniques could be the starting point for in-depth exploration of woven structures. I hope that you will be encouraged and inspired to use them in this way for discoveries of your own. There is a certain magic in weaving something useful or beautiful from an armful of natural materials, even more so if you have collected that bundle yourself. You may have harvested and graded your materials, or they may be processed commercially, but, when woven, they will always retain much of their original identity, and a natural quality which is instinctively appealing and warm.

About the Materials

Plant fibers divide into types which have specific techniques and geographical areas associated with them. For instance, artifacts from grassland areas of Africa are significantly different in construction from those traditionally made in temperate European forests or areas of tropical rain forest. Soft materials, like rush, lend themselves to plaiting and coiling while harder materials, like willow, are more suited to frame and rib, or stake and strand techniques. Cane provides both long flat strips of chair cane from its outer skin and a harder core. Wherever you are, look out for materials to harvest which will be suitable for plaiting, lashing, or weaving.

Making the Projects

The projects range from a very simple spiral plant support, to large complex articles which require skill and several days to make. For anyone who has not worked with these materials before, it is best to begin with a project that does not need large a investment in tools or materials. Read right through the project you want to make. Familiarize yourself with the techniques and tools. The projects contain instructions for weaves specific to them, but you may also need to refer to the techniques chapter for general weaves. These are indicated in the projects by page numbers. If the materials require a long soaking time, make sure you prepare enough. Take your time: weaving is not a speedy craft.

Learning More

I hope that you will take ideas from this book, and, by making changes in scale, color, or materials, create your own pieces. One of the best ways of learning is by observation. Keep a notebook and a tape measure, with you and draw, or write down how things you see are made. If you have enjoyed making the projects, joining a basketmaking class or group is one of the best ways of continuing to improve your skills.

Photograph: Liz Crossley

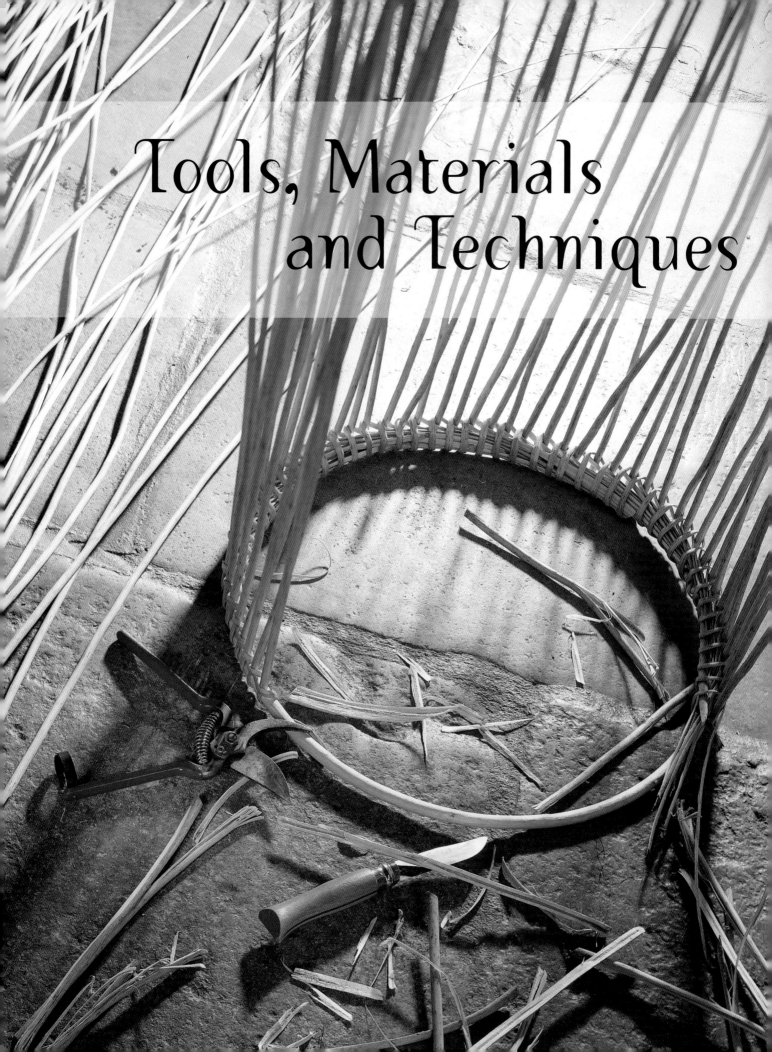

Tools, Materials
and Techniques

Tools

This section on tools tells you how to go about using them. Do not forget that your body is one of the tools you have to work with and don't push yourself beyond your capabilities. Weaving something you are pleased with takes practice and concentration. The larger projects require physical strength and stamina which can only be built up over time.

General Tools

Most of these are tools you may have already if you are interested in craftwork, otherwise they are widely available.

A **wooden yardstick (1)** or meter rule, is not essential but extremely useful for quick measurements. Because it is not flexible it is easy to use across a piece of woven work and you can run it up and down to check accuracy. A **flexible tape measure (2)** can be used instead.

To check levels over a distance or maintain a straight edge a small spirit level can be held against the wooden rule.

A small **hand drill (3)** is needed for some projects. It has the advantage of not needing a power supply and of being quiet. You may prefer to use an electric drill.

A **vise (4)** or Workmate is essential if you have to clamp work steady. **G-clamps (5)** are sometimes useful for specific projects. A Workmate can double as a handy screwblock.

A mister/spray bottle of the sort used for houseplants will help to keep your work damp. You will also need to find for various projects; a selection of buckets and bowls for soaking cane and bark, tape, string, rope, nails, pins, glue, varnish, brushes, scissors, and weights.

For dyeing cane you will need to have some old saucepans, metal spoons, and plastic gloves that you do not use for other domestic purposes.

You will also need old cotton towels and/or sacking to keep your materials damp and for mellowing after soaking.

GENERAL SAFETY

• Secateurs will cut your fingers if they are in the way. Hold the secateurs slightly away from your body, since the handle ends can nip too.

• DO NOT use a utility knife, because the blade is too short, or a craft knife because the blade is too thin and flexible. Also, never cut toward yourself with a utility or craft knife.

• Bodkins and awls are potentially dangerous tools. Never use them toward yourself, or over your leg or hand. You have to push fairly hard to use them and they can very quickly pierce right through your work, or slip and make a nasty puncture wound. DO NOT leave them lying on the floor: bodkins will roll, sending feet flying.

1

2

3

4

5

Cutting Tools

You will find these by searching out good hardware stores and those which sell garden equipment, or sports shops that deal with hunting and fishing.

To cut cane you will need a pair of **sidecutters (6)**. These will snip cleanly through the cane and cut close to your work. I have found that a tool used for bonsai, a small **branch cutter (7)**, is very suitable. It has a sharp cutting edge at an angle. This makes it useful for trimming ends inside curved shapes such as frame baskets. It is also strong enough to cut through willow.

You may also need a pair of **round-nosed pliers (8)**, which are used to kink cane without cutting through it, and also to pull a length of cane through your work.

An essential tool that you will use frequently is a pair of **secateurs (9)** or hand-held pruning shears. Try not to use them for general garden work because they need to have clean-cutting, undamaged blades. The most suitable type are the ones that have a bypass blade (the two parts of the blade slide past each other) and not an anvil type (where one sharp blade cuts down onto a flat surface). With the former you get a smooth clean cut and with the latter the material tends to be crushed. Of course, they must be kept really sharp.

Ideally you should have two pairs: **fine-bladed secateurs (10)**—which are light but strong for smaller work where the thinner blade will cut into the smallest spaces—and strong heavy secateurs for cutting through large material.

If you look at the blades from both sides, you will see that one side is flat, while the other side has a raised edge. Always lay the flat side against your work when you cut. It is small details like this that will give your work a good finish.

If you are cutting through very heavy material, tuck the rod under your left armpit. Cut with your right hand, and lever down with your left hand on the end you are cutting off, to take some of the strain. If you are left-handed, just reverse the procedure.

If you are interested in gathering your own material, especially heavier sticks, a pair of **loppers (11)** are a good investment. Once you have a pair you will wonder how you managed without them. The long handles give a lot of leverage and they will slice through with very little effort and save your back too. As with shears, bypass, not anvil, blades are better for this job.

A small **pruning saw (12)** with a folding blade is not essential but very useful if you intend to gather your own material. It can also be used like an ordinary saw when you get the material home. Otherwise a small tenon saw is necessary for some projects.

A good knife is essential. Most basketmakers and chair seaters have their own favorite type and you should find one that is right for you. It should have a **fixed blade (13)** or a **lockable blade (14)** that will stay in place once open. The blade should be 3–4in/7.5–10cm long, strong, with good rivets and not thin or flexible. Suitable knives are available in shapes that vary from crescent to straight, and some are straight with the tip curved slightly outward.

They are available from specialist suppliers, except for a French knife with a folding blade, which has a locking ring, which may need to be sourced from mail order outlets.

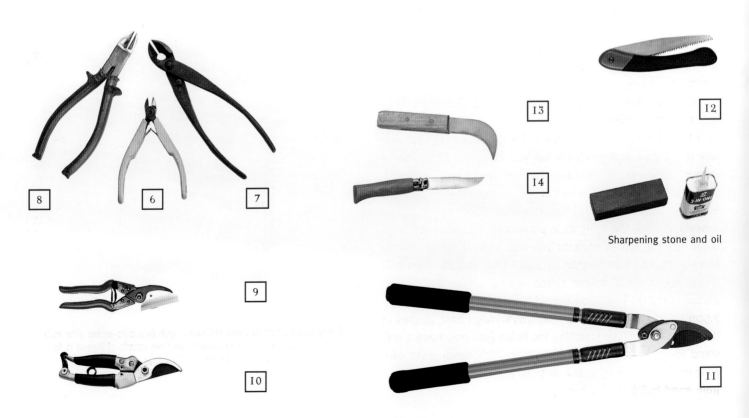

Sharpening stone and oil

Specialized Tools

These are tools commonly used by basketmakers. You may have to order them from specialist suppliers, or even have them made. Build up your collection slowly, as your skills progress. If there is a range of sizes to choose from, start by getting the tool that is the most generally useful size.

You will need a **bodkin (15)** or two. This is essentially a large awl with a sharp point, and gradually becomes thicker. Its main function is to open a space in the weaving to allow you to push another weaver in or through. Bodkins vary from thin to very thick and a medium-size one, about 6in/15cm long and $\frac{1}{2}$in/1.5cm diameter, is very useful if you are going to have only one. You will also need a small awl for finer work.

The bodkin is often used in basketmaking, together with tallow (an animal fat) into which it is dipped to grease the way. Tallow is often difficult to obtain, and vegetarians do not like to use it. Soap will do the job: grate some into an unbreakable container with a little water.

Rapping irons (16) are used to compact the weave while working with willow and gathered material. You should develop the habit of using yours frequently, every few rows. There are various designs and they usually weigh from 8oz/225g to 2lb/907g. Some have one edge beveled to allow them to rap into narrow gaps. A thin fitching iron is used to work between closely set stakes. A ring at the handle end of a metal rapping iron is useful for straightening curves in large sticks. Push the stick through the ring and lever gently against the curve, moving along the stick. A good general-purpose rapping iron weighs 1lb/450g and should be 8–10in/20–25.5cm long.

Wooden rappers (17) do not crush and tear the bark when working with "unstripped" materials. They need to be made from a heavy wood, Box for example, to be effective, or the weight can be increased by drilling down the length and filling it with lead or metal bars.

When you work with rush you need a **rush threader (18)** to pull the soft rushes through without damaging your work. A rush threader has a narrow, rounded end and a wide eye. This tool is not commonly available but you can fashion one from a loop of thick wire, or purchase one from specialist suppliers.

A **screwblock (19)** is used in some of the projects. Basketmakers use a screwblock to make the bases for square baskets. It holds the uprights in place while you weave through them. For the screen projects you will need to make a large screwblock. Use two lengths of wood (this can be sawn and unplaned), longer than the screen you will make; I used two 4ft/1.2m lengths. The wood should be fairly heavy 3 x 3in/7.5 x 7.5cm or 2 x 4in/5 x 10cm is fine. Drill through both lengths in three places, carefully matching the holes (you may need a drill stand to get straight holes). Join them with coach bolts with wing nuts, or, less costly, saw in three a threaded bar (available from good builders' merchants;

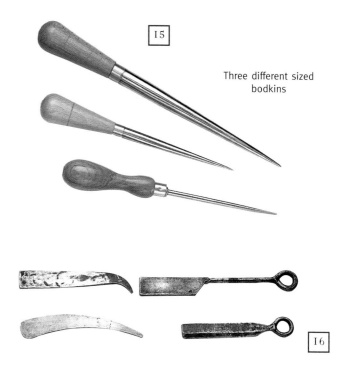

Three different sized bodkins

Four metal rapping irons of various weights. Two have rings at the end for straightening rods. At bottom left is a fitching iron

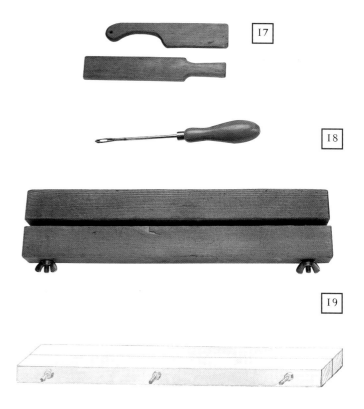

Either coach bolts or threaded metal with two nuts either side with wing nuts to prevent movement. Make sure length of thread is long enough to accommodate thick sticks in the center

I used a bar ³⁄₈ in/1cm in diameter, just over 3ft/1m long. Screw on the nuts and washers before cutting. A small screwblock needs only two bolts.

You will need a **tank (20)** for soaking willow. A galvanized tank at least 6ft/1.8m long and about 2ft/60cm deep is best. Cut two lengths of wood tight to the inside width to act as wedges to keep the willow underwater. It is possible to improvise with plastic sheet and bricks to make a temporary tank, especially if the bundle you are soaking is not large. An old bathtub will do, but tannin from the bark will stain the enamel if you use your regular tub. Buff is the worst for this—wrapping the willow in a towel while soaking will help to prevent staining. A barrel or drum is not usually tall enough to accommodate the willow, although you can soak one end and then the other. A plastic drainpipe with one end plugged takes a small bundle of rods.

To make skeins in willow you will need special skeining tools—a **cleave (21)** to split the rod in three or four, a **shave (22)** (to take the pith from the back), and an **upright (23)** (to even up the sides)—these have been designed to make uniform skeins. The adjustable blade of the shave is used to take layers of the pith progressively off the back of the skein. The upright has two angled blades which can be altered to cut the edges of the skein to a uniform width.

If you need to make only a few skeins for lashing, or if you wish to make chunky split rods for weaving with, you can manage without an upright and a shave. The tools you will need are a three-way cleave, a sharp, straight-bladed knife, and some **leg protection (24)**. The usual cleave is oval, narrowing to a three-part blade at one end. An easy cleave to use is one in which the splitting edge is sunk below the top edge of the tool so that the rod is driven evenly forward.

Chair-seating Tools

Some tools designed specifically for chair seating may be obtained from suppliers.

A **clearing tool (25)** is used to knock out the old cane and pegs from the holes. Turn the chair upside-down to do this, so that you drive the pegs out the way they were knocked in. This makes the job easier and prevents damage to the frame. This tool can also be used when inserting new pegs to knock them down flush with the frame.

A **shell bodkin (26)** is useful when working the weaving stages in caning. When working near the edge of the frame it helps to slip the curved tool under the canes where you need to weave. The working cane can be slid into the channel in the tool, and is pulled through more easily.

For rush seating there are specialized tools available. These can also be improvised. A rush threader is used for seating and rush basketmaking (see above). Rushes are threaded through the eye and pulled through the work without damaging the materials. A **wooden stuffing stick (27)** is used to push waste rush deep into the corner pockets of the seat to pack it firm while you are seating it. It is a smooth thin stick with a thin rounded end.

To smooth the seating coils you use a **wooden dolly (28)**. This is worked over the coils from the outside of the seat into the center, while the work is still damp, using an ironing motion to bed the coils down level with each other.

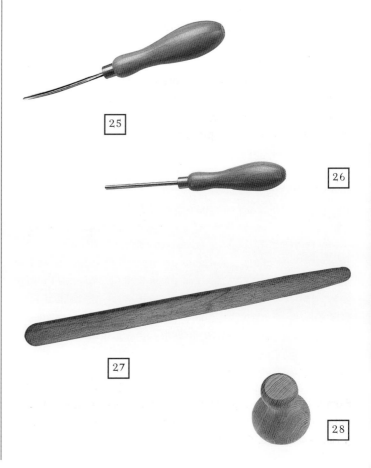

Materials

Cane, rush, and willow are the main materials used in the projects in this book. How each material is prepared for use is described here, as well as other materials such as straw and seagrass. Materials may also be gathered from the garden or wild. What to look for and how these are prepared and used is explained here.

Cane

Several hundred species of the Calmoideae family, generally known as Rattan or Cane, are found in the tropical regions of China, Indonesia and Malaysia as well as in Africa and Australia. It is a palm which grows like a climbing vine. The stems, which rarely reach a diameter of more than 1¼in/3cm, climb and trail to lengths ranging from 65ft/20m to 600ft/180m by means of the hooked thorns on the stems, and the long feelers which are found at the ends of the fronded leaves. Most of the cane available commercially comes from Indonesia, where it is dragged out of the forest by hand, and it is also farmed in "rattan gardens" along the banks of rivers. From planting, it will take 13 years before a garden is in full production.

The word wicker is a general term usually meaning any pliant twig which can be used for weaving.

HARVESTING AND PROCESSING: Wearing thick leather gloves, the stems are chopped through with an axe and the thorny bark left to shrink until it can be removed by pulling it through a notch cut into a tree trunk. It is cut into long 'poles' and transported to central warehouses. From here it is exported to be processed, usually to Singapore or Hong Kong. Once it has been washed, the outer layer is split off to produce chair cane using rollers to press it against knives, then the inner pith is driven through cutters to produce center cane or reed.

From left to right: 1 Lapping cane and chair seating cane. 2 Whole rattan. 3 Round center cane in two sizes. 4 Dyed round center cane. 5 Flat center cane. 6 Dyed flat cane.

Chair Cane

The layer under the bark, which is hard with a shiny surface (from the silica in it) and looks as though it has been varnished, is sold as chair seating cane. Stripped off the stem, in lengths between 10–20ft/3–6m, it is sliced lengthways into specific sizes from about ¹⁄₂₀in/1.5mm through to ⅕in/6mm.

Chair cane names and sizes US	Equivalent sizes UK
Carriage 1.5mm	0 = 1.5mm
Superfine 1.75mm	1 = 1.7mm
Fine Fine 2.25mm	2 = 2.1mm
Fine 2.5mm	3 = 2.5mm
Medium 3.0mm	4 = 2.9mm
Common 3.5mm	6 = 3.5mm

The size you need to use is worked out by measuring the number of holes across an average 6in/15cm, in the frame of your chair. Use the following guide to help you select the right size of cane, but be aware that holes are not always drilled to accommodate the right size cane. Where two sizes are shown, use the wider one for the diagonal weaves. Beading is usually done round the edge of the seat in No. 6 cane.

No. of holes per 6in/15cm	CANE SIZES US	CANE SIZES UK
15	1.75&2.5	1&2
14	1.75&2.25 OR ALL 2.25	1&2 OR ALL 2
13	2.25&2.5	2&3
12	2.25&2.75 OR ALL 2.5	2&4 OR ALL 3
11	2.5&2.75/3.0	3&4
10	2.75&3.0 OR ALL 3.0	3&4 OR ALL 4

PREPARATION: merely dampened with a cloth. The hard surface is virtually impervious to dyes, but can be stained to match old cane using wood stains.

Center Cane or Reed

This is processed from the pithy center of the rattan. The whole length is driven through knives which cut it into round, flat, or half-oval shapes of varying sizes or widths. I have specified several sizes in the projects, but because the difference between sizes is so small, one size up or down will not make a noticeable difference.

American	British	Metric diam.	
3	4	2.25–2.50mm	Round cane
3½	5	2.5mm	Round cane
5½ or 65	12	3.75mm	Round cane
6 or 6½	14	4.25mm	Round cane
3/16in		4mm	Flat oval reed
¼in		8mm	Flat reed
3/8in		10mm	Flat reed

Flat cane will have a right and a wrong side. Bend the damp cane around your finger and you will find that the fibers on the wrong side will split away while the right side is smooth.

A cane gauge, a flat plate with holes in it, can be used to determine the sizes of round cane. Cane is imported into America and Europe from Indonesia, in several qualities, but it is becoming an ever more expensive material and should be used sparingly. The destruction of the forest to provide land for crops will put more pressure on the supply. Cane is sold by weight in bundles, some craft shops will sell small quantities.

PREPARATION: Porous center cane readily absorbs water. Wind lengths into manageable loose coils and soak them in a bowl of water. They will need 3–10 minutes depending on the size, but do not oversoak them or they will discolor and the grain will be raised, making them rough. Hot water will speed up the process. Wrap them in a damp towel when you take them out, and keep them covered while you are using them. They can easily be dried and resoaked, so do not prepare more than you need at one time. If you leave damp cane in a warm place or in a polythene bag it will go moldy.

Dyeing Cane

Center cane dyes well and evenly. Dyes suitable for cotton fabrics will work well. Cold-water dyes will give light colors; hot-water dyes are more effective, giving deep rich colors. Fiber-reactive dyes react with the cellulose fibers and yield bright colors. Wet cane appears very dark. Remember that the color will be much lighter when dry. Wind the cane into loose coils and soak in warm water first to ensure an even take-up of the dye. Prepare the dye bath and add the cane. Keep it moving in the dye for the first 10 minutes to distribute the dye evenly.

Follow the instructions on the dye packaging. Remember that dyes are potentially poisonous, so take sensible precautions. It is also possible to color small quantities of center cane using wood stains (preferably water-based). Brush or sponge them on. Chemical dyes should be treated with care. Wear plastic gloves and protect yourself and your clothes.

Rush

English rush is the true bulrush, *Scirpus lacustris*, not the plant with the brown furry seedhead which is known as reed mace, or cattails in America. It grows in slow-moving rivers. Look out for the small inflorescence of brown flowers at the top of the stem. Rushes are smooth, without nodes, and round (unlike sedges, which are triangular), bright green and grow up to 8ft/2.4m tall. Inside they have a spongy structure running lengthways, which makes them both soft and strong lengthways, but they can be easily torn or broken across the stem.

Cutting takes place in late summer from a flat-bottomed boat. The rushes are still green but the growing season is over. To cut the maximum length, a hook is dragged through them several feet underwater, then the cut bundle is pulled up and out and they are carefully laid flat on the boat. Any kinks will cause cracks, which will leave points of weakness, where they will break off when they are being used.

The bundles are taken to the river bank, sorted, and tied into a loose bundle. They are dried standing up, and well ventilated, to prevent them going moldy and spotted (although some spotting can be attractive). They will slowly dry to a pale-green color, which will fade to a yellowish brown. Keep them away from the light to retain the green color. If you find rushes growing and you would like to harvest them, you must ask permission from the owner or the relevant rivers authority before you can help yourself.

English and Dutch rush can be bought from commercial suppliers by the bolt (a large bundle measured by the diameter at the thick end).

PREPARATION: The thickness of the rushes in your bolt may vary. Sort the narrow ones for chair seating. The larger ones will do well for braiding, or plaiting.

Rushes will take up water into their spongy centers very easily. Do not soak them. Lay them flat and sprinkle them using a watering can with a fine rose, turning them so that the bundle is evenly wet. Wrap them up (the best results are obtained from doing this overnight) to mellow in a well-wrung-out, damp blanket. When you unwrap them they will be soft and pliable. They do retain air, which can be squeezed out if you handle the rushes firmly as you coil, plait or weave. Damp rushes have a wonderful smell. Prepare only as much as you can use in a session, because they will quickly go moldy. Dampened rushes can be dried out completely and reused.

Willow

Over 300 species of willow (genus: *Salix*) are found in the temperate regions of the northern hemisphere, thriving in damp conditions. Over the centuries varieties with characteristics that make them suitable for basketmaking (long, pliable, slender rods) have been constantly selected for propagation.

The first year's growth is the most pliable and useful. In the second year the rod will branch. Every year in winter, all growth is cut back to the ground, yielding rods of varying lengths. Willow from commercial growers in Europe can be obtained in its dry state, in three distinctly different types:

Brown is any willow with its bark on, even though the color can vary. The type most commonly sold is the variety Black Maul, which is greenish brown. Flanders Red, a harder, rust-colored willow, and Whisender, which is stouter, straight, and more springy, are sometimes obtainable. Brown willow has a more rustic look than the next two. Sometimes steamed willow is available. This has the bark on but it sheds easily, and the color is shiny black/brown.

Felicity Irons, rush merchant and basketmaker, harvests her rushes on a river in Bedfordshire, England. The rushes are cut, lifted, and then stacked flat on the boat.

From left to right: 1 "Green" fresh-cut willow. 2 Brown willow. 3 White willow. 4 Buff willow. 5 Dyed willow.

Buff has been boiled with the bark on. Color and tannin permeate the rod and turn it warm reddish brown. After this the softened bark is stripped off. The processing makes it easy to use and hardwearing.

White has had the bark peeled off to expose the inner rod. It is not possible to do this easily until the sap begins to rise in the spring and there is a gap between the bark and the rod. After this a "second skin" develops and the two are welded together again. Growers cut in the fall and artificially keep the rods alive by grading into bundles and "pitting" them in shallow tanks of water. Stripping is done by passing them through a machine with rollers that look like a mangle.

Buying Willow

Willow is sold in Europe in bolts; a large bundle which is measured by diameter (37in/92.5cm) at its thick end. The rods have been graded into lengths, available from 3ft/90cm upward to about 8–9ft/2.4–2.7m. Belgian willow is sold by the kilo (2.2lb), graded from 39in/1m and then every 4in/10cm to 78in/2m. English willow is imported and is available in the USA by weight in imperial measurements. Thick sticks, which are the result of allowing the rods to grow on for a second year, are sold in buff and white.

Bolts of 3ft/1m and 8ft/2.5m brown willow stand waiting to be loaded into the brick boiling tank. Processing for buff is carried out in the spring. A fire is kept constantly stoked and the willow is kept underwater for three hours. A lift gantry is used to hoist the hot bolts out.

Bolts of willow stand 9in/22.5cm deep in concrete pits until they begin to show signs of life (buds breaking.) They are then "peeled" and "stripped for white."

PREPARATION: Sorting the willow in one bolt into various sizes is called *cutting out*. You can pick out the various sizes you need from the bolt as you go along, but it is far better to sort the whole bolt as soon as you cut the ties. To do this, lay the bolt with the butt ends facing you, work through the bundle dividing them into two sizes, putting thicker rods to one side and finer ones to the other. When you have two piles, repeat the process with each one. You will then have four bundles of

well-graded rods ranging from thick, to medium, to fine. It takes time to become used to the fractional differences in diameter of the material. With practice this job will not take you long and is well worth the effort. If you are a beginner this is one of the best ways of getting a feel for the sizes which will make such a difference to the quality of your work.

Soaking

All willow bought dry must be soaked and mellowed before use. You will need a tank, or you can improvise (see Specialized Tools page 11).

The longer the rod the more time it will take to soak. Brown takes the longest because water has first to penetrate through the bark. Exact times are difficult to give because of the variable factors. Cold water will slow the process; conversely, warm (not hot) water will certainly speed it up if you are in a hurry. Essentially the rods must take up water until they are wet through. Less than this, and they will crack when woven; too much and they will be soggy and split when you use them. Think of spaghetti and aim for *al dente*.

Test to see if it is "done" by bending a rod over at the butt end. It should not crack. Sticks will take several hours to soak but usually do not have to be bent in more than a gentle curve. Skeins and split willow should just be dipped and wrapped in a damp towel.

A rough guide to soaking times

length	buff and white	brown
3ft (90cm)	½–1 hour	2–3 days
4ft (1.2m)	¾–1½ hours	3–4 days
5ft (1.5m)	1–2 hours	4–5 days
6ft (1.8m)	2–3 hours	5–7 days

Mellowing

This is the second part of the preparation process and equally important. Surface water is driven off and the core of the rod mellows, making it supple. After removing the rods from the tank, wrap them in a damp towel or sacking which has been well wrung out. A large old cotton blanket is good for larger material. Synthetic materials are unsuitable, as they do not hold water in the same way. Leave them for several hours or, better still, overnight. They should remain covered until you use them.

Buff and white willow will not remain in good condition for more than a day or two before becoming greasy, and soon after will develop mold. This happens especially quickly in warm weather. If you are not going to use them in time to prevent this, dry them out and resoak them later. Brown willow will last a lot longer damp, but will also go moldy in time. The bark will shred if you soak it more than once.

Dyeing Willow

It is possible to dye white willow bright colors, and dyeing over buff willow will give earthy colors. This is easiest using fiber-reactive dyes, and can be done in a plastic drainpipe with one end plugged. Fill the upright pipe with dye and water mixed following the supplier's instructions. Immerse the willow for several hours to take the color. Dry—then rinse well. Small amounts of willow can also be dyed with a wood stain (water-based), using a sponge and gloves.

All chemicals should be used with care following the manufacturer's safety precautions.

If you can find a farm where LIVING WILLOW is being grown for biomass (large fast-growing species burned to provide power) you may be able to buy it in its green state. Willow of this size has become very popular for making living structures and sculptures. All willows have the ability to root from every part of the stem (a process known as totipotency), essential in their role as a pioneer species, being one of the first to colonize wet areas. This means that freshly cut willow can be pushed 6–8in/15–20cm into the ground, and if you keep the area weed-free and damp, it will be sending up fresh shoots the same year.

Living structures need maintenance and have to be pruned annually, otherwise the cuttings will grow into trees. Be careful not to site these structures near drains.

From left to right: 1 Colored bark willows. 2 Dogwood. 3 Ash. 4 Palm. 5 Hazel. 6 Elm bark.

Gathering Materials

It is possible, and inspiring, to gather your own materials from the woodland or hedgerow. You just need to know what to look for. Once you have an idea of what you would like to make and have had some experience of weaving with natural materials, your eyes and hands will be "tuned in" to the feel and scale of what you can use. Of course, you must ask for permission to harvest from whoever owns the land.

The time to go hedgerow gathering is in the fall and winter. Once the leaves have fallen, the sap will stop running and the material will be much more pliable. If there is a frost, so much the better, since this will speed the process.

What to Look For

The rods you collect should be long and pliable. The first year's growth is best for this, so what you cut should be at the end of the branch. You can tell where one year follows another, because there is a marked change in texture and size in the material. The current year's growth has no lateral shoots. Side shoots grow out in the second year.

Try bending the rod in a gentle curve. If there is too much pith you will soon tell, because it will snap and when dry there will be no substance to it. Some plants do not have the right structure and will kink rather than curve.

The rod should be long in relation to its width at the butt end, and slender.

Woody Varieties

The DOGWOODS (genus: *Cornus alba*) have beautiful colored bark, green and red in the wild and ranging from bright-red (*westonbirt*) to green (*flaviramea*) and black (*kesselringii*) in garden cultivars. Look for HOLLY (genus: *Ilex*) growing in the shade where it will send out longer trailing shoots from underneath. At first bright-green, it goes black when dry. SNOWBERRY (genus: *Symphoricarpos albus*) dries to a pale gray. Elm (genus: *Ulmus*) is very pliable. BLACKTHORN (*Prunus spinosa*) dries a plum color.

HAZEL (genus: *Corylus*) is soft brown in color in its first year but older wood has a striking silvery bark. Young SYCAMORE (*Acer pseudoplatanus*) and SWEET CHESTNUT (*Castanea sativa*) make good hoops for frame baskets. WILLOW (genus: *Salix*) is the easiest material to weave and is found in the wild in many different varieties including common osier (*Salix viminalis*), which is large-growing, and goat willow (*S. caprea*), which is tough and orange/purple colored. Willows favor wet marshy land, as does ALDER (genus: *Alnus*), which has a similar pliable quality but is more branching with attractive violet buds and a purple-gray bark.

Some trees produce suckers which provide a good source of easily harvested material, such as, LIME (genus: *Tilia*) and PLUM (genus: *Prunus*).

PREPARATION: Once cut, there is usually still too much sap left for you to use freshly gathered stuff immediately. Even if you can bend it, it will shrink a lot. Leave it for three to six weeks outside in a shady place out of the wind. It will slowly become more pliable and less cracky. After this, use it before it dries out too much. Some materials such as, willow and hazel can then be resoaked (see page 16) but not more than once.

Red dogwood, *Cornus alba*—each year one-third of the shrub should be cut out at the base to promote the brightly colored new growth. The prunings yield good weaving material.

Climbers, Grasses and Leaves

Many climbing plants produce suitable weaving material: hops, Virginia creeper (which has interesting nodes and tendrils), the older wood of honeysuckle (boiled to remove the bark, revealing a creamy, smooth center), and grapevine prunings are all possibilities. When you gather them, wind them in coils and put a tie around them.

Flat materials, suitable for braiding, should be gathered at the end of the summer. Being softer and on the whole annual plants, they die down early. Plants to try weaving with include flax (*Phormium* from New Zealand, not the Irish sort), *Crocosmia*, Iris (especially the flag iris with long leaves, which grows in wet meadows), and cattails.

Palms of all types have very strong, fibrous leaves, good for knotting. Grasses are delicate with ears that add texture to weaving. Collect them early before they shed seeds everywhere.

All soft materials need to be collected in quantity because they compress on weaving. Dry them spread out in a warm place with good ventilation if they are not to go moldy. To preserve maximum color do this away from the light. Once dry, tie in bundles. Most will require only dipping in water and wrapping in a towel for a few hours before use.

Bark

Some species of trees have bark which is suitable for weaving with. The best time for removing bark is in the spring and early summer, when the sap is running. Bark can be removed from willow and also briar (wild rose) once you have removed the thorns. Score it with a knife lengthways and pull it off in a long strip. Coil in a roll with the outer bark to the inside. Dry in a warm place before it goes moldy. Other species are worth experimenting with. The bast (inner bark layer) of certain trees (lime, elm, sweet chestnut) can also be collected.

Collecting Bark for Seating

Firstly, we need to be clear what we mean by "bark" seating. The material used is correctly known as "bast" or inner bark, which, before it dries, is very much like leather. This is the layer beneath the relatively rough outer surface that you can see when looking at a tree. However, as bark is a better-known word, I shall continue to use it.

In Europe, there appears to be no tradition of using bark for seating, although it was widely used in the making of rope. Its use is best known in North America where European settlers must have learned the techniques of weaving bark from Native Americans and adapted these techniques for use on the ladderback chairs that they brought with them. The main species of tree used was hickory, renowned for its toughness.

In Britain, experiments with all the possible native species have found the best to be wych elm (*Ulmus glabra*), although bark from the various species of lime can also be used despite being less flexible. It is easiest to harvest during the growing season of spring or early summer. This is when new wood cells are being formed, creating a soft, moist layer between the bark and the wood. You should look for a fairly small tree about 4–12in/10–30cm in diameter with a straight trunk and as few branches as possible.

Fell the tree (always have permission of the landowner) and remove the smaller branches up to 2in/5cm diameter, taking care not to cut or bruise any of the bark that you intend to use.

Using the draw knife to remove the outer bark

Support log at either end above the ground

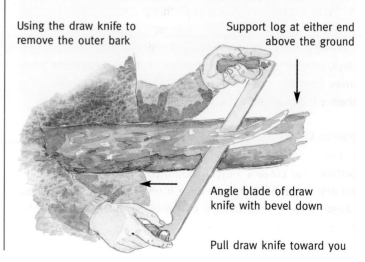

Angle blade of draw knife with bevel down

Pull draw knife toward you

It is possible to use bark from the larger branches but generally it is easier to concentrate on bark from the main trunk. If possible, remove the bark from the tree on site to avoid having to haul large logs with the danger of damaging both the bark and yourself. The bark strips should ideally be from 7–13ft/2–4m long, so cut the tree into suitable lengths. To create a comfortable working position, support the logs at around waist height while removing the bark.

Apart from the saw already used to fell the tree, you will need only two other tools: a draw knife and a knife, both of which need to be kept really sharp. Starting at the butt end of the log, carefully remove the crinkly outer bark with the draw knife, revealing the pale, soft, inner bark beneath. You should notice that, within a few minutes, this inner bark will have turned brown, just as an apple does after being peeled.

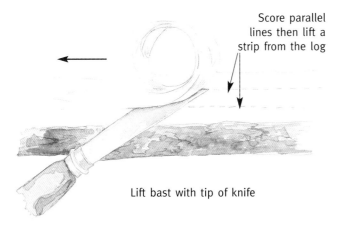

Score parallel lines then lift a strip from the log

Lift bast with tip of knife

Removing the inner (bast) layer with a knife

Having completed this stage, take your sharp knife and cut the bark into strips about 1in/2.5cm in width. Try to feel for the flow of the grain while cutting these strips to maintain its maximum strength. When you come to a branch you have three options:

1 If the branch has not been removed, you may be able to run the strip along it;
2 You can swirl the strip around the branch;
3 You can terminate the strip at that point.

Provided that you have harvested the tree during the growing season and that you remove the bark within a few days, you should be amazed how easily the strips can be lifted away from the wood beneath. Roll the strips into coils, tying them either with string or with small slivers of waste bark.

PREPARATION: If you intend to use the bark within a few days, it can be stored in cool, moist conditions—under leaves for instance—to prevent it drying out. If you have to store the bark for any length of time, then hang it up in a dry, well-ventilated situation to dry out quickly before it can develop any mold. Make sure that the coil is not so tight as to prevent air circulating over the complete surface of the bark.

Other Materials

SEAGRASS is a twisted two-strand cord made from a type of sedge (*Carex*). Sedges have triangular stems and grow in wet areas, either meadow or on the shoreline. If you have access to the materials, you can make your own following the instructions for cordage on page 45. Otherwise, it is commonly available in craft shops, sold as a chair seating material. It comes in hanks and does not appear to have a standardized weight or thickness. Dip it in water and wrap it in a damp towel to mellow for half an hour before using it.

STRAW should be hand harvested into sheaves if it is to be used for any sort of weaving. Straw which has been compressed into bales will be too damaged to use. For straw plaiting, only the top section of the stem, above the first node is used. For this sort of work the crop is a specially grown, long-straw variety. Wheat straw is sometimes sold in craft shops for "corn dolly" work. If you live in an area where cereal crops are grown you may be able to obtain a sheaf cut by hand, before the crop is machine harvested. Oat straw is specially golden in color, and rye straw is long and very fine. To prepare it you should merely dip it in water and wrap it in a damp towel for an hour.

RAFFIA is the fiber stripped in lengths from the underside of the large raffia palm leaf. The fiber is long, narrow, soft, and extremely strong. One end is thinner and tougher. If you use raffia to sew or coil with, you should thread this end through the needle so that the fibers do not shred. It is sold in hanks, either in its natural color, or dyed. It takes dye well and can come in very bright colors. It is sold in craft shops, although natural raffia is often cheaper in garden centers. Use a spray mister to dampen it and wrap it in a damp towel before using it.

Techniques

This chapter on techniques contains instructions on general weaves, and those techniques which are common to several projects. If you already have some basketmaking skills, you will find weaves that you recognize here, and hopefully some new and interesting ones to try out. If you have not done any weaving of this sort before, read and practice this section carefully.

General Weaving

The weaves are described as if working in willow. For cane work, ignore the references to tips and butts.

Shaping your work: The most difficult part of weaving in three dimensions is getting the shape you want. It takes time and practice to feel confident with the materials. The shape is achieved by the position of the stakes or uprights; these are held in place by the hand position you adopt when weaving. Hold the stake you are working over between the thumb and forefinger of your left hand. As you place the weaver in position put your thumb on the weaver, locking it in position against the front of the stake. The right hand puts the weaver in place, but should not pull on it. The kink that you make with the weaver is crucial to the shape, keeping the stake in position.

COMMON TERMS

Rod—one year's growth of willow

Tip—the thin end of the rod

Butt—the thick end of the rod

Stick—thick material usually cut from the butt end of the rod or stout material

Upright or stake—the rods that are set up to make the sides or "warp"

Stroke—one movement in the weave

Slype—slanting single or double cut made in the butt end of a rod

Skein—narrow, ribbon-like length, split from a willow rod with the pith shaved off

Kink—a bend made in the rod when weaving or turning down the stakes into a border

Pricking down—kinking the stakes to turn down the border OR pushing weaving rods into previous weaving to secure them or hide the ends, then bending them ready to weave

The correct hand position during general weaving

A NOTE FOR LEFT-HANDED BASKETMAKERS
All the instructions and projects are described with a right-handed person in mind, that is, working from left to right. It is much easier for a left-handed person to work right to left and there is no reason why this can't be done, but for reasons of space it wasn't possible to include reverse instructions in this book.

A general rule for weaving is that you should start and finish a section on the tips of the weavers to avoid jumps in size that will leave gaps in your work. Some weaves and techniques do not follow this rule and this will be indicated. When using willow, aim to even up the effect of the taper of the rod by carefully matching the sets of rods you are working with, and joining, in most cases, the tip ends to tip ends, and butts to butts. The sets of rods should work together.

When you make a join, replace all the rods in a set consecutively in the spaces between the stakes. Do not be tempted to carry one of the rods on because it is longer, or you will end up with the stronger rod pulling the weaker one out of shape. Always use up the butt ends of your weavers as this is where the strength of the rod is. However, you should be aware that if weavers become stronger than the uprights, they will bend them out of shape, your work will look unbalanced, and you will find it a struggle to weave.

Small adjustments in the position of the stakes make large differences higher up. Keep an eye on the final position of your stakes, since it is difficult to pull them back into shape later. Aim to have them evenly spaced and making a smooth surface, with no significant "hills and valleys."

With some weaves (**randing** and **slewing**) you need to count the number of stakes you have before you start. (This does not apply if you are weaving from side to side, for example on a screen.) If there are an uneven number of stakes the weave will be correct when you come back to the beginning and you can just continue to weave. If there are an even number of stakes the weave will not work out—you will be constantly weaving under and over the same stakes. In this case you should start a second set of weavers on the opposite side of your work, making sure that they make the opposite movement to the first set. The two sets will chase each other in a spiral but do not cross over each other.

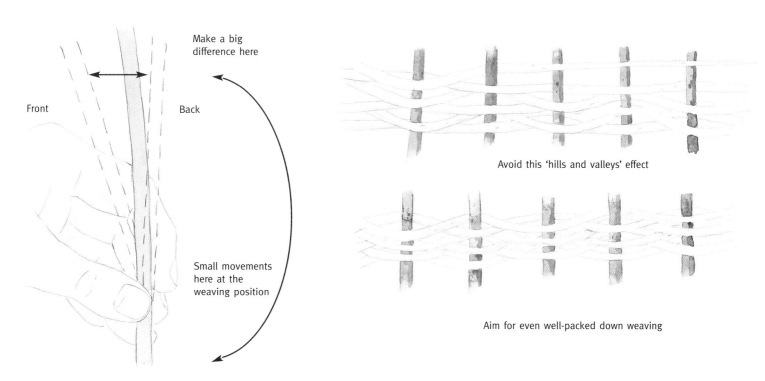

Make a big difference here

Front   Back

Small movements here at the weaving position

Avoid this 'hills and valleys' effect

Aim for even well-packed down weaving

Weaving with One Element

Randing

This is a simple over-and-under-one weave with a single rod, cane or other element. It can be started with tips or butts depending on its purpose. There are two ways of joining:

1 Joins are butted up: tips to tips or butts to butts.

2 A pieced-up or overlapping join.

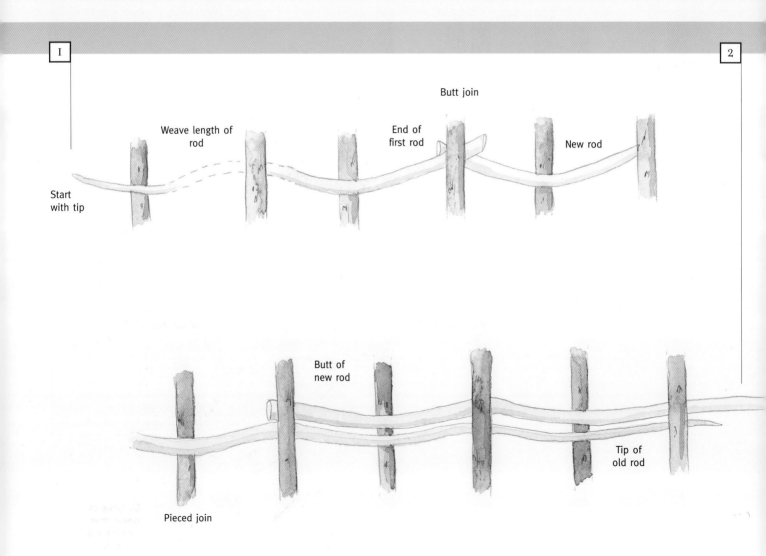

Start with tip

Weave length of rod

End of first rod

Butt join

New rod

Butt of new rod

Tip of old rod

Pieced join

Packing

Use this technique to build up a section or block of weaving, by weaving extra rows across the selected stakes.

1 Simple block: For a straight-sided block, work backward and forward over a set of stakes. To keep the weaving level you can wrap twice around the end stakes.

2 Frame baskets need to be packed in a way that will not leave obvious gaps. Do not pack on the same ribs twice. With flat cane, twist as you pack to keep the right side of the weaver on the outside. This is not necessary when weaving with whole rods.

1

2

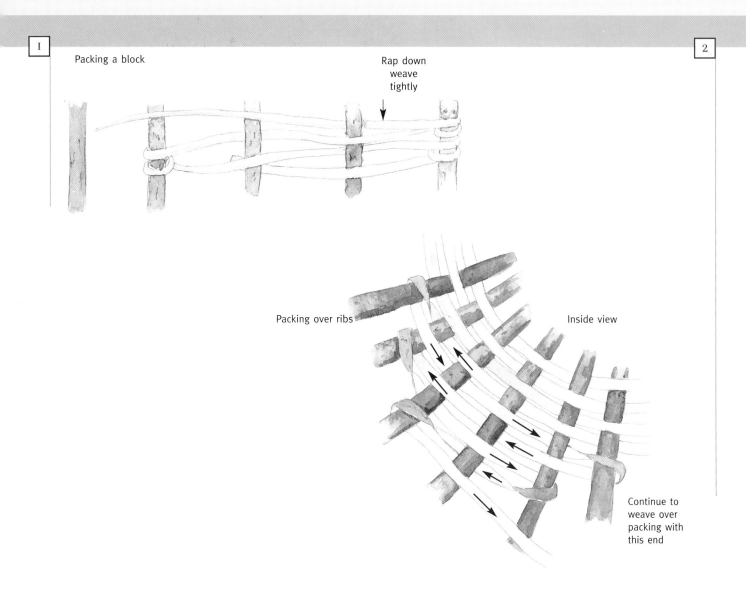

Packing a block

Rap down weave tightly

Packing over ribs

Inside view

Continue to weave over packing with this end

Weaving with Two Elements

Pairing

This is a strong weave using two rods, useful as a beginning row in a piece of work. Two weavers ply over each other, left OVER right, alternately. They must be well matched or the weave will be unbalanced. For pairing with a double twist see the conical plant support project, page 110.

1. You can start with two butts, or two tips pushed into consecutive spaces.

2. Alternatively, overlap the tips and work the rods double for a few strokes.

3. **Pairing can be joined in several ways:** A simple butt join (tips to tips or butts to butts). Join a new rod 1 and weave one stroke, then add in a new rod 2, and weave. Trim ends later.

4. A crossed join which is more secure (tips to tips or butts to butts). Push a new rod 1 into the "notch" at the back, and underneath old rod 1, then weave one stroke with rod 2.

5. An overlapped join (butts over tips), see diagram 3 on the Coracle project page 124.

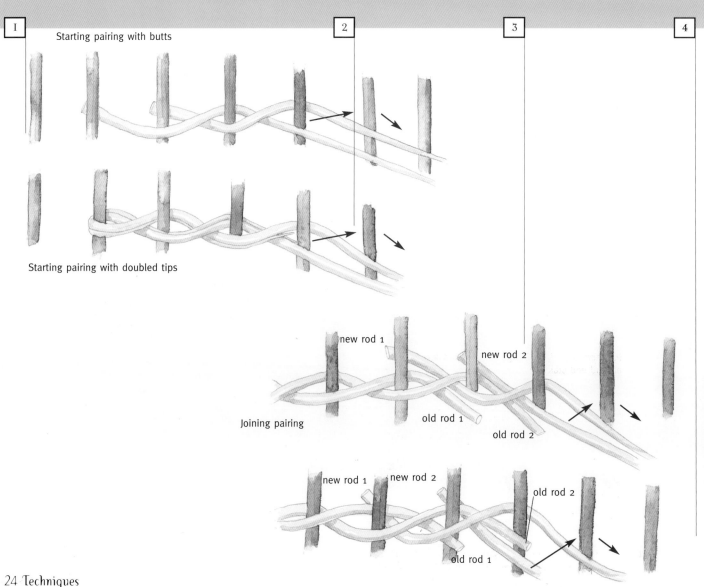

1 Starting pairing with butts

Starting pairing with doubled tips

2

3

4

Joining pairing

new rod 1

new rod 2

old rod 1

old rod 2

new rod 1 new rod 2

old rod 2

old rod 1

Pairing to Start a Screen

A single twisted row of weaving is needed at the start to keep the stakes in place and to prevent the finished weaving from slipping off the end.

1 Measure on the rod from the butt end, twice the width of your screen and then place the weaver into the space between stake one and two at this point.

2 Bring the tip end round and pair to the right. At the right hand side bring the heavier end of the rod back to the left using a randing weave.

3 Then bring the finer end of the rod back to the left until it runs out. Use a randing weave to continue the screen.

1 **2** **3**

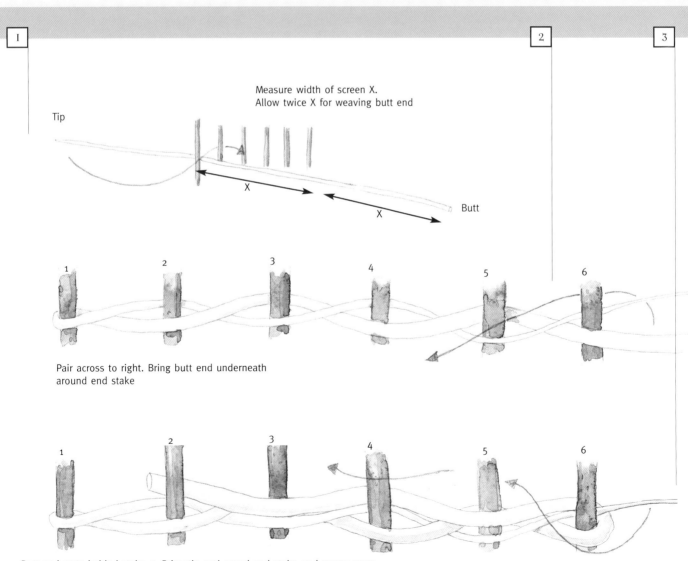

Measure width of screen X.
Allow twice X for weaving butt end

Tip

X X Butt

Pair across to right. Bring butt end underneath around end stake

Butt end rests behind stake 2. Bring tip end round end stake and weave away.
To continue, start randing with new butt end of rod overlapping tip

Fitching

This weave is added to a band of openwork or stakes to hold them in place. It is often used when stakes are scallomed onto a frame (see Cutting Scalloms on page 36). The gaps between the stakes must be very narrow, the width of the rods themselves. Fitching gives an open but strong weave and looks superficially like pairing. However, the technique is completely different. The twist is left UNDER right (opposite to pairing). You will need to work with two well-matched rods.

1 Start by kinking the first third of both rods from the tip ends and fold them back to double with the opposite rod. This maintains an even weight along the length of the rods.

2 Wrap the rods around the first stake and hold the two equal ends in your right and left hands, so that they grip them with the backs of your hands upward. Your hands must remain this way up all the time.

3 Bring your right hand OVER your left, and at the same time slide your left hand to the back UNDER your right.

4 Insert your right index finger in the gap (to lock the weave into position and act as a temporary stake). Let go with your left hand, and use it to take over from your right.

5 Use your right hand to take the weaver behind the next stake and press it into position firmly with your thumb. Both sides of the fitched weave must have equal tension to obtain the desired effect. Grip the loose weaver with your right hand so that you are back at step 3.

6 Repeat steps 3, 4, and 5.

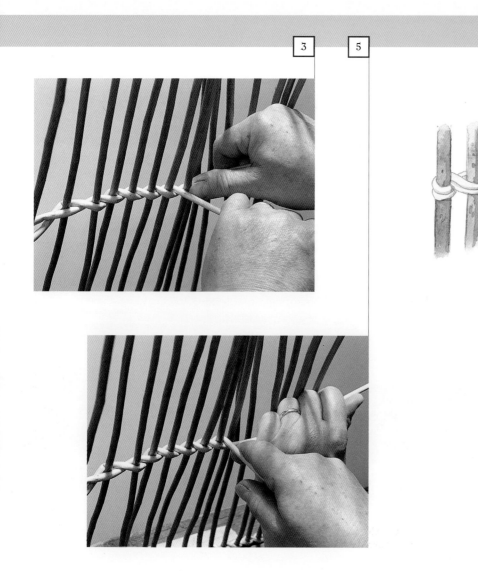

Double tips run out

7 How to join fitching: Add new rods butt to butt, matching to the existing size. Do not make joins in consecutive spaces. Lay the new butt on top of the one you are replacing when it is coming from behind a stake. Take both rods to the front, flick the old butt out of the way and make the normal movement with the new rod, pulling it extra tight to avoid a bulge.

8 To join tips to tips: Lay in new rods and work double for the last third of the old rod to maintain an even weight of weaving.

9 To complete the fitch: Overlap the beginning by several strokes and then thread the two ends down into the lower fitch.

10 Trim all ends to ¼in/7mm once the work is complete and the stakes are unlikely to move.

This traditional French design for a chicken coop shows how a row of fitching keeps the stakes tightly together. *Jan de Vos.*

7

9

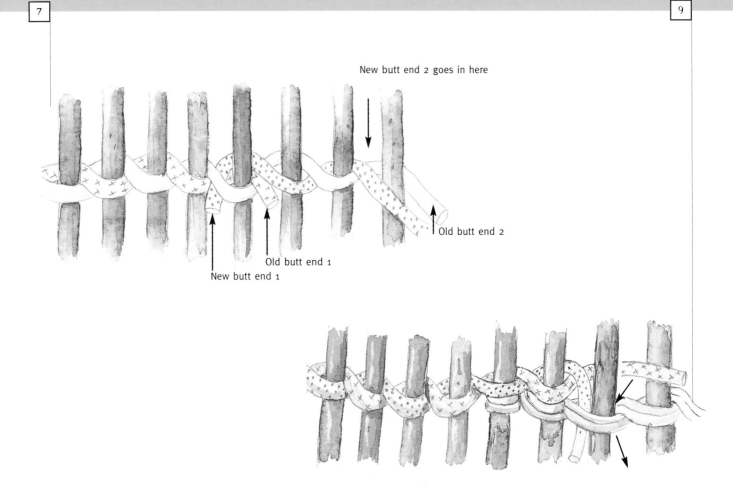

New butt end 2 goes in here

Old butt end 2

Old butt end 1

New butt end 1

Completing the fitch: overlap the lower weave for several strokes.

Weaving with Three Elements
Waling

This is a strong weave using three rods which helps to control the shape of your work well. It is used when you need to change the direction of the stakes or make a firm band of weaving.

I Start with three tips in consecutive spaces, and, always using the weaver on the left, weave in front of two stakes and behind the next one.

2 **How to join waling:** To join butts to butts, slide the new weaver into the front of the old one. Work one stroke. Then do the same with the second and third new weavers. Join tips to tips in the same way.

3 **A stopped wale:** This weave is used when the wale finishes at two edges rather than working around continuously, for example on a screen. Start by wrapping a spare rod around the outside stake on the left, as if there are two weavers in position. Another spare rod makes the third weaver. It can either

be laid into the space between stake three and four OR it can be pricked down next to the first upright (if you do not want an end showing on the back).

4 Weave to the right as for normal waling. The two ends of the first rod will quickly become uneven (one thick, one thin). Replace them by joining new rods by the butt ends (see step 2) to match the second rod you used. When you reach the right-hand side the weavers have to be woven around the right-hand side to complete the wale.

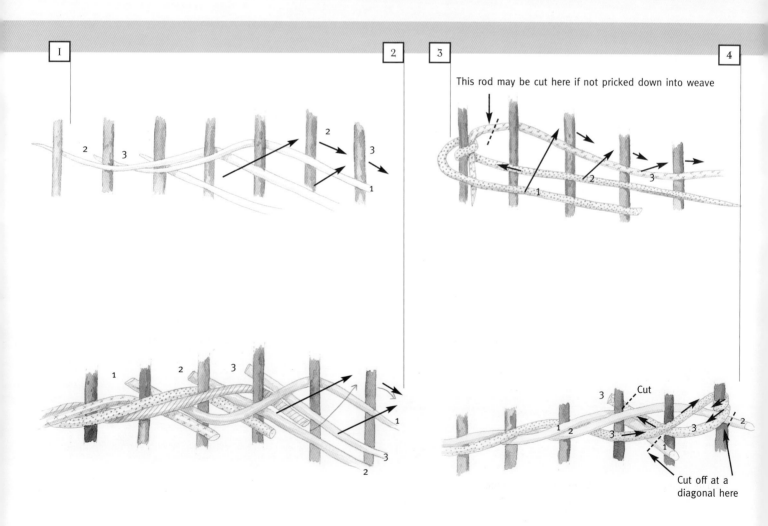

I

2

3 This rod may be cut here if not pricked down into weave

4

Cut

Cut off at a diagonal here

Slewing

This weave is quick to do and similar to randing but using three rods at the same time. As you work with the weavers forming a strong band, they will quickly pull your weaving out of shape if you do not keep them slender. Use your left finger and thumb to control the tension.

1 It is a simple over-one-under-one weave. Start with a single rod, putting the butt end behind the stake. Weave for a third of the rod, then add the second rod, by the butt end, on top of the first. Weave them together for another third and add the third rod.

2 When you have woven another third the first rod will run out. Add the next rod on top by the butt end, in the space that you drop the first one. Slewing can be worked with more than three rods at a time. The more rods you use the wider the band of weaving will be and the more difficult to control. Over an even number of stakes you must use two sets of weavers.

1

Slewing, weaving the first three rods

2

new rod

Adding a new rod as you drop the one at the bottom

REVERSE WALING

You may want to have two bands of waling (on a screen or chair seat). You can either turn the weavers around the right-hand edge and work back to the left instead of finishing them off as above (this is rather untidy and it is difficult to get the rods to wrap around the end stake in a neat sequence), OR start a complete new band of waling, this time working from the right to the left following the directions for the stopped wale. This will give you a neat arrowhead pattern where the two bands meet. (This is not a true reverse wale, which would be worked from left to right, in front of two stakes and behind one, with the weavers running under each other instead of over.)

Weaving with more than Three Elements

French Randing

A very neat weave in which all the weavers start at once, usually with the butt ends, and work out to the tips. Before you start, count out and make sure you have one weaver for each stake (or space). This weave works to the LEFT.

[1] Insert a weaver with the butt braced against the stake, work one stroke to the right. Insert the next weaver by the butt, to the left and repeat.

[2] Do this all the way around, until you have two weavers left. These must go in sequence underneath the starting weavers.

[3] **To weave:** Each row is complete in itself. Start anywhere and work one stroke to your left with each weaver. The first two will immediately make doubles. When you come back to the doubles again look under the weave to make sure you use the two lower ones in the correct sequence.

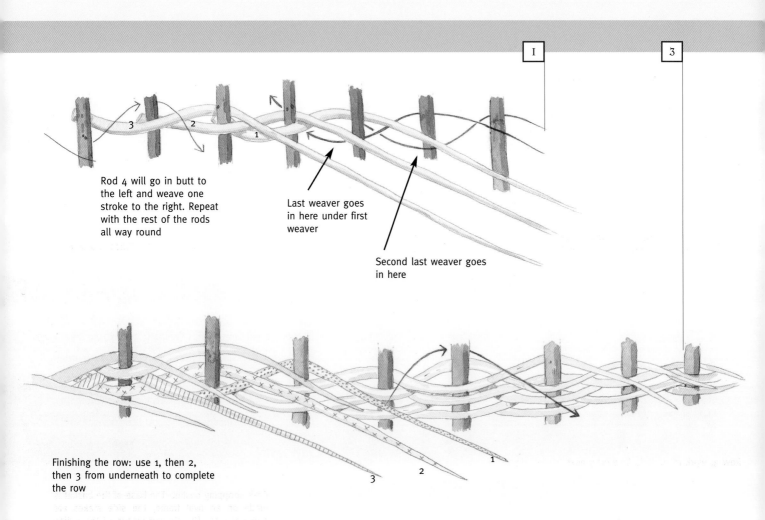

Rod 4 will go in butt to the left and weave one stroke to the right. Repeat with the rest of the rods all way round

Last weaver goes in here under first weaver

Second last weaver goes in here

Finishing the row: use 1, then 2, then 3 from underneath to complete the row

Zig Zag Weave

This is a very decorative weave. I call it Eva's Weave, because she is the person who showed it to me, but it is also known as Zamba. The stakes must be strong and straight and evenly spaced for it to look good.

Each stake has an accompanying weaver (or two weavers: if you work it double it will fill twice the space vertically). The rows work alternately to the left and right so you must remember to change the direction you weave in on each row.

1 Set up and work the first row as for the start of French randing (working this first row to the left).

2 On the second row, work moving to your RIGHT, folding each weaver back on itself behind the stake on the left.

3 The third row is like French randing, again moving to your LEFT. Continue to repeat the second and third rows, working out to the tips of the rods.

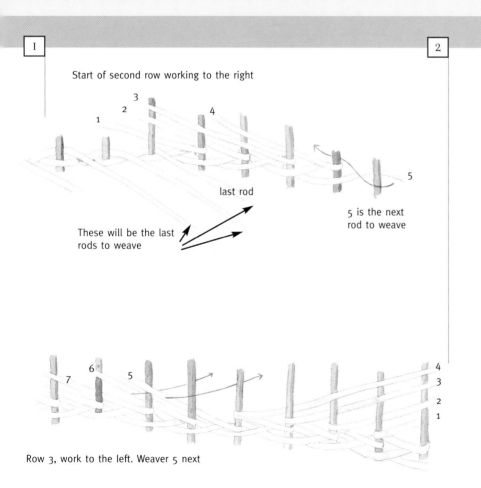

Start of second row working to the right

last rod

These will be the last rods to weave

5 is the next rod to weave

Row 3, work to the left. Weaver 5 next

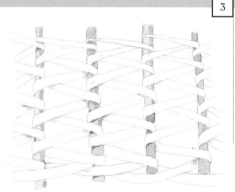

Finished weave

Eva's shopping basket: The base of the basket is made on an oval frame, the side stakes are scallomed on. The zig zag weave of the siding uses doubled weavers; the flowing shape is achieved by weaving these doubled sets to varying heights.

Trac Borders

These are simple borders which can be woven with several variations. The first stake kinks down to the right and weaves diagonally down, in front of and behind the next stakes, to meet the last row of weaving. Each stake on the right follows in turn, making the same pattern. The last stakes kink down and take their place in the wedge-shaped gap left by the first stake.

The height of the border is determined by the number of strokes each weaver makes. Measure and kink all the stakes at the right height carefully before you start.

1 Start of a trac in front of one behind one x 4. This border is used in the project for the Sentinel Lantern, and it can be seen in progress there.

2 Finishing off the trac border. The last stake completes the pattern. Kink into sections before weaving away.

3 **Variations:** The trac can be worked in front of and behind more than one stake at a time, creating distinct ridges, or it can form a very simple edging as shown in the diagram.

I   2   3

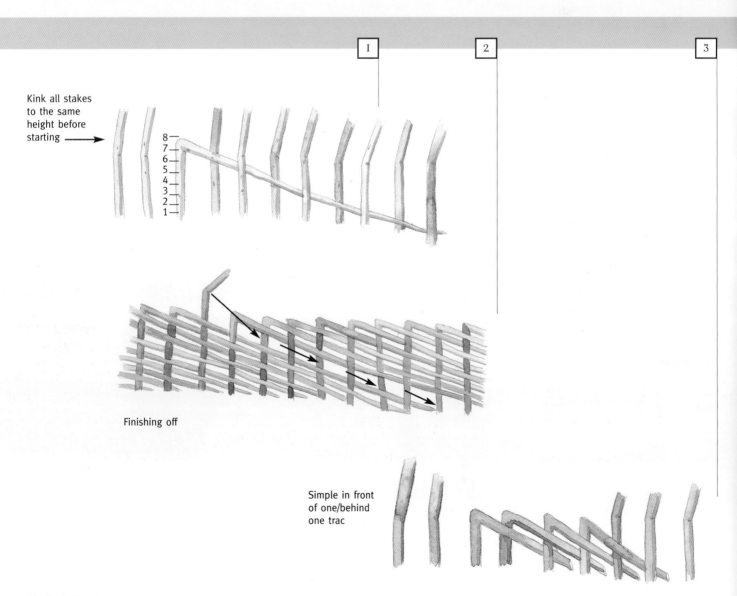

Kink all stakes
to the same
height before
starting →

8
7
6
5
4
3
2
1

Finishing off

Simple in front
of one/behind
one trac

Finishing Off

Willow needs no special finish, and should not be varnished. Trim all loose ends close to your work using shears. Make sure that the end of each rod rests against a stake so that it is braced. Use the shears flat against your weaving, (see secateurs p.10) making diagonal cuts. If you cut French randing rods too short they will pop out of the weaving, leaving gaps.

When you have trimmed all the ends run your hands over your work. There should be no snags, but ends should be neither too short – when they will undo or too long – when they will break off.

Willow may become brittle in heated houses and should be given a good soaking from time to time to revitalize it. Items left outside will degenerate quick and the application by brush of linseed oil mixed with a little turpentine will make them more durable.

Cut cane so that it is braced against a stake, with side cutters or branch cutters at an angle. Any white ends that show against dyed cane can be touched up with color marker pens. Cane is slightly fibrous and there may be untidy ends which are too fine to cut off. These can be carefully singed off: Give the work a good soak and then run it quickly through a gas flame, turning it constantly, being very careful not to set it alight or blacken the weaving.

When properly dry, cane can be given a finish of matt polyurethane varnish to bring out the color. This will also prevent it from fading. Rush and soft materials should be tidied up by trimming all loose ends closely using scissors.

Trimming ends of borders: The end must slightly protrude past the spoke over which it is lying so that it does not unravel.

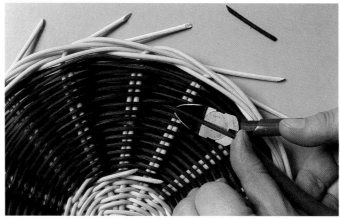

Trimming the ends of weavers: Trim with the flat end of the sidecutters against a stake so that the work is braced.

Splitting Materials

The principle of splitting is the same whether you are splitting in two, three, or more. You must keep an even tension on each of the sections, or the split will run off across the grain to one edge. You alter the direction of the split by putting tension on the opposite side (the side that is thicker). Do this by pushing on your knife, or cleave toward that side, as you work along the rod or stick and you will see the split run back to the center.

Once you have started to split the rod, you no longer need a sharp blade, because the split will run ahead of the tool you are using.

1 Start the skein by cutting away the tip of the rod at an angle with a sharp knife. Bend back the top edge with your thumb. You will see a "V"-shaped notch on the lower edge.

2 Insert the cleave into this and push down on the rod. Hold the rod with your left hand under the cleave, and work down the rod to the butt end.

3 All the pith now has to be shaved off the back of the skein, or it will not be supple. You need to protect your thigh with a leather pad that will not slip. First shave a section of pith from the butt end so that you can grip the skein with your left hand. Placing the skein face down, hold the knife at a shallow angle and press downward. Do not dig into the skein. Pull the skein toward yourself through the blade of the knife, keeping the knife still. Work your way along the skein.

4 When it is smooth and pliable, hold it up and run the knife along both of the edges to make it a uniform width.

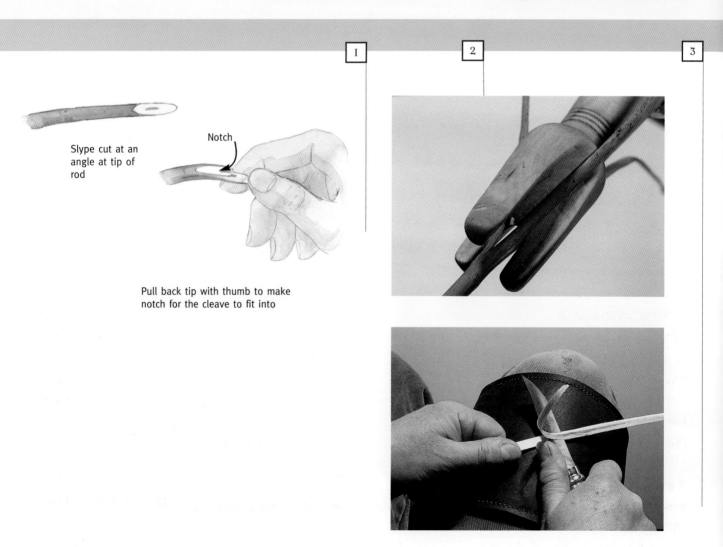

Slype cut at an angle at tip of rod

Notch

Pull back tip with thumb to make notch for the cleave to fit into

Making Hazel Skeins

In spring and summer, when the sap is running, narrow lengths of bark can be lifted, with a sharp knife, from fairly slender rods of hazel that have a diameter of 1in/2.5cm upward, avoiding the effort of felling a much larger tree.

1 Having cut the rod down, bend it carefully round your knee, or a solid curved form such as a post, to stretch the fibers.

2 Insert the knife blade flat and lift a section the width you want, $\frac{1}{4}$–$\frac{1}{2}$in /0.5–1.5cm is a good size. You will find that a skein will split away from the core, along the grain.

3 Pull it up and then move along the rod, bending and lifting as you go. You may be able to lift several skeins off the same rod, if there is enough tension left in it.

4 Run your knife along the sides of the skein to trim off any rough edges. Use it immediately or store it coiled loosely with the bark facing inward to dry. Soak it before using.

3

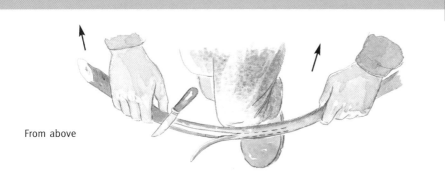

From above

MAKING CUTS

Always keep your knife well sharpened, this helps to make clean cuts. To cut willow or gathered material to a point (a slype) basketmakers traditionally make the cut toward themselves with a fixed or locked blade. This is contrary to all that you have been taught about safety (see page 9), but it is the quickest way to prepare your material, and, provided you do it properly and do NOT use a utility knife, because the blade is too short, or a craft knife because the blade is too thin and flexible, you will find that it gives the best control over the shape of the cut.

Grip the material with your left hand under the rod, with fingers and thumb on top, lock your left elbow against your body. With your right hand make the cut, keeping your thumb UNDER the rod. The blade should remain just behind the thumb and not forward of it, so that knife and thumb cannot meet. Pull toward your right with the knife, keeping your elbow locked and moving from the shoulder. Your right elbow can only travel backward a short

distance before it locks, not far enough to reach your body, so you should not cut yourself. You need to make the movement with some confidence to cut clean through the material first time. The cut (slype) you are aiming for should be flat and clean with a sharp, hard end

Slypes, cut single and double

so that it slides easily into your work without snagging. It can be a single cut or make two cuts so you have a double edge.

Cutting Scalloms

A scallom is a long tail cut on the butt end of a rod. By paring away the pith, the part left is flexible enough to use as a wrap. Scalloming is a way of attaching rods to a frame. The tail should be long enough to wrap around and along the frame, to be caught in by the following two scalloms.

1 **To cut a scallom:** You should already have had practice cutting toward yourself with a knife. Brace the butt end of the rod against your chest, so that it is bending slightly under the tension. Holding your hands in the positions shown, cut into the rod. Keep your thumb under the rod and the knife level with your thumb.

2 Cut a curved section down into the rod and then along toward yourself and lift up the pith. Move your thumb BEHIND the piece you are lifting off.

3 Slide your left thumb down to brace the tail at the back and lever off the top half all the way to the end. Keep equal pressure on top and bottom with your thumbs to prevent the split running off. Clean off all the pith with the knife, and leave a tidy end which is not too thin.

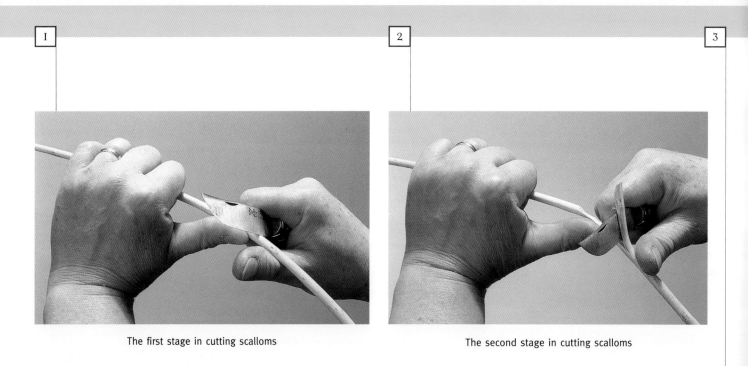

The first stage in cutting scalloms

The second stage in cutting scalloms

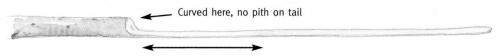

Curved here, no pith on tail

This section to be very flat and pliable, as it wraps around the frame

4 **Using scalloming to start the weaving:** Cut scalloms on the butt ends of all the rods that are going to be attached to the frame by placing the tail end inside the frame and bringing it up and over the frame, and then around itself to the left. Wrap them on with the curved cut tight up against the frame. Each successive scallom holds the previous ones in place. When you come round to the beginning again, cut the last few tails shorter, but make the very last one long and weave it away on top of the start.

5 An alternative way of finishing off is required when working across a discontinuous frame. (See Willow and Rush Stool project page 96, diagram 2).

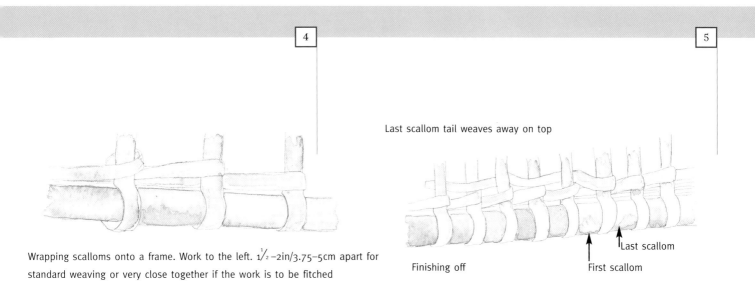

4

Wrapping scalloms onto a frame. Work to the left. $\frac{1}{2}$–2in/3.75–5cm apart for standard weaving or very close together if the work is to be fitched

5

Last scallom tail weaves away on top

Finishing off

Last scallom

First scallom

HINT
Scallom rods onto the frame holding it between your knees and pushing each rod in toward the center to keep the tails tight.

Frame Techniques

Interesting structures can be made using frames as the outline shapes. Frames are used in the construction of baskets where the frame supports the weave and ribs are inserted to fill the gaps. To make the frame soak your dry rods well so that they are pliable.

Another option is to use material that has been cut "green" and then allowed to dry out to a "semigreen" state (three to six weeks) so that it is pliable but will not crack or kink. It is a good idea to make your frames in the fall and leave them tied in shape to dry for later use. Dried in this way they will not be so liable to lose their shape while weaving. Hoops are made by bending stout rods into a circle.

Usually you will be using material that is thicker at one end than the other. You must work harder to curve the thick end or it will kink at the thinner end, at the spot where there is most pressure (the shoulder on an oval).

Making Frames

I   Work on the rod with both thumbs underneath, pushing up to stretch the fibers on the top of the curve and bending gently. For a large oval frame you sometimes make two half-hoops because the taper of the rod will make it too thin at one end to make a strong frame. In this case bend the rod carefully into a curve and tie across the two straight ends with string and allow it to dry in shape.

I

Frame basket with hand holds woven in and shaved white willow. *Lee Dalby.*

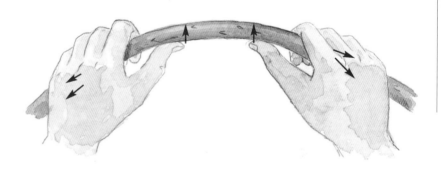

Push up with your thumbs while levering down and out with your hands. Work your way along the rod bit by bit from the butt end

2 You can curve the rod following its natural form, or, to put more tension in it and make it stronger, bend it against the curve. To help you make the shape you can use a specially made mold or find something solid and curved to bend the rod around. I have found a large empty gas cylinder excellent for this. Hold the butt end of the rod hard against the former with your left hand, and pull the rest of the rod around the curve with your right hand. Square frames can be made with thick, well-mellowed willow, kinked around nails, which are hammered into a plank in the desired shape (see White Willow Lantern project page 68). "D" shapes are made using a combination of these two techniques.

3 **Joining frames**: The two ends of a frame must overlap in a neat join. Bring the two ends together and mark on each one the length of the overlap. It should be 5–8in/12.5–20cm long. The butt end should be on the outside. The inside edge of the butt end is shaved, as well as a short length on the outside-edge to bring the end to a thin taper. In addition to this, take off a slight amount along the sides to match the diameter of the other end of the rod. On the thinner end you should do the opposite. A little of the outside of the rod is shaved off and a short length on the inside.

4 **Lashing the join together**: Use a willow skein or chair seating cane. Pinch the end of the skein upside down in the center between the two overlapped ends. Wrap toward the right, pulling the two halves of the join together tight and catching in the shaved end. Wrap back all the way over to the left end, making crosses on the outside of the frame.

5 Complete the join by wrapping back to the middle and threading the skein back next to where you started. Use a bodkin to make a space for this.

6 **Notched join**: An alternative join is to make the shaved sections much shorter with notches and grooves cut at either end. Tie these very tightly with strong, nonstretch twine, wound around several times to bed it down.

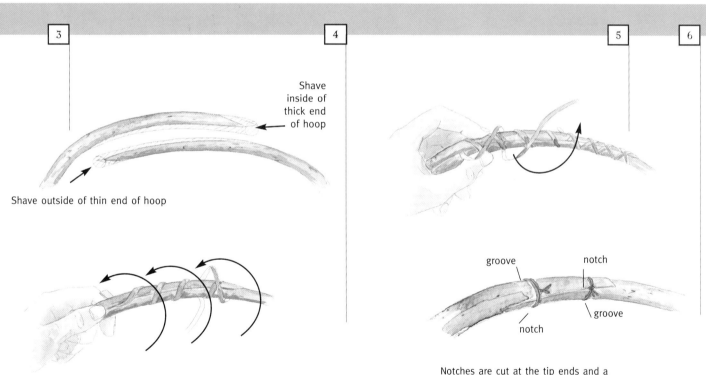

3

Shave inside of thick end of hoop

Shave outside of thin end of hoop

4

5

6

groove   notch

notch   groove

Notches are cut at the tip ends and a corresponding groove made in the opposing rod

Wrapping and Binding

CRANKING WILLOW RODS

This is a difficult technique to explain and teach, but simple to do once you know how. It is a knack that will come with practice. By twisting the fibers of the rod into a spiral, you can make it so flexible that it will act like a piece of rope. First attempts usually result in mangled, shredded rods, because the fibers separate too much.

The butt end must be firmly anchored so that it will not swivel. You can either anchor it in the weave, under your left foot, or in a vise. Hold the rod just down from the tip end in your right hand and about 8in/20cm down in your left hand.

Begin to wind your right hand in a circle away from you. At the same time press down with your left hand to maintain tension on the rod. As you put twist into the rod, the fibers give. You will feel this, and may hear it too. Allow the twist to run down through the section in your left hand (if you pinch the rod too tightly at this point it will kink).

Now slide your left hand down the rod, follow it with your right hand, and repeat the action until you reach the butt end of the rod. The section you have cranked will unravel. It is easy to twist up tight again when you weave or make a wrap with it.

A Simple Wrap

To make a simple willow wrap to hold a bunch of rods together:

1. Hold the rods to be wrapped in your left hand.

2. Use a slender, mellow rod and hold that in your hand as well, with the butt pointing upward.

3. Wrap the rod around the bunch several times tightly.

4. Trim the tip to a point and thread it back through the wrap next to the butt end. Use a bodkin to make a gap. Pull both ends tight. If you are using large rods you may need to crank them to make them pliable.

5. A wrap can be both decorative and functional, as this wrap holding crossing rods together shows.

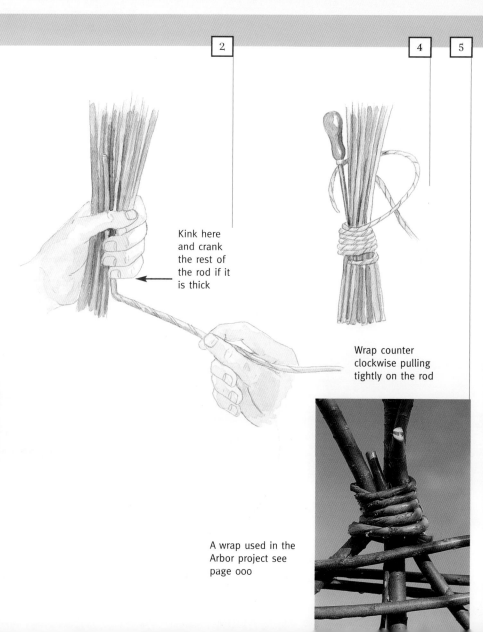

Kink here and crank the rest of the rod if it is thick

Wrap counter clockwise pulling tightly on the rod

A wrap used in the Arbor project see page 000

Wrapping along a Rail

This technique is used when wrapping the rails of a chair before weaving a seat or for wrapped handles. You can use whole rods or flat materials, such as skeins.

1 Start the rod with a tip end and wrap over the tip, or anchor it into previous weave.

2 To join: Make all joins in the underside. Push in the butt end of a new rod (it may need to be shaved down). Link the two rods before continuing the wrapping with the new rod over the end of the old one. Bulky joins can be flattened by tapping gently with a hammer.

Making a Tie

This type of tie is used to prevent weaving slipping, for example, on the top border of a screen.

1 Slype the butt end of a rod and insert it into the weave to the left of the border stake. Crank it well. Wrap it over the border and under the weaving several times before weaving it away to secure it.

2 Or, wrap around the middle of the tie twice before threading the end away, to make a butterfly tie.

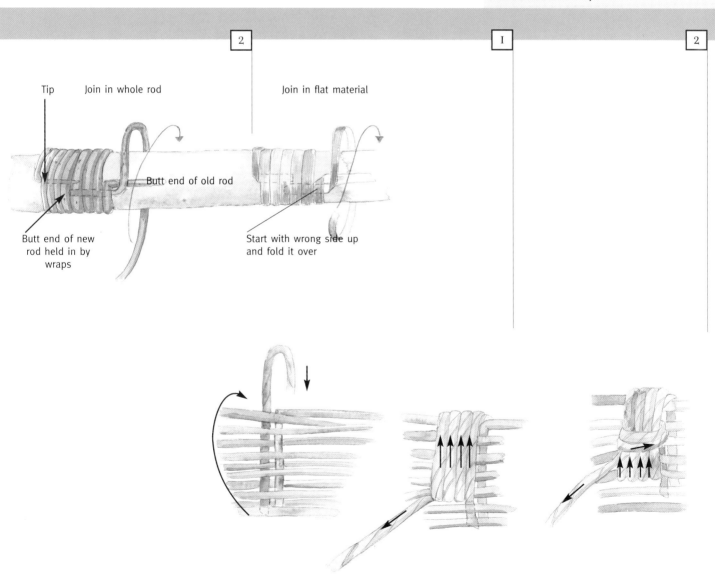

Tip   Join in whole rod

Join in flat material

Butt end of old rod

Butt end of new rod held in by wraps

Start with wrong side up and fold it over

Making a God's Eye

Also known as a four-fold bond or four-point lashing. This binding technique and other variations, suitable for tying ribs into frame baskets, are found both in Europe and Mexico. It is a circular lashing which wraps each rib in turn, working counter clockwise. It is usually worked using flat materials, such as flatband cane.

1 Start the god's eye by wrapping diagonally across the center at the point where the two frames meet. Wrap from bottom left to top right and catch in the tail at the back under the first wrap.

2 Follow the diagram working in front of and behind each rib. Always cross diagonally counter clockwise on the front.

3 **Joining on:** If you use willow skein you may need to make a join if the material is not long enough. To do this tuck the working end under the previous wrap. Begin a new skein by pushing it firmly under the old end as far as it will go. Continue to wrap with the new length in the usual direction.

4 **To finish off:** Tuck the end under the last wrap to keep it in place. The tail is held in by subsequent weaving.

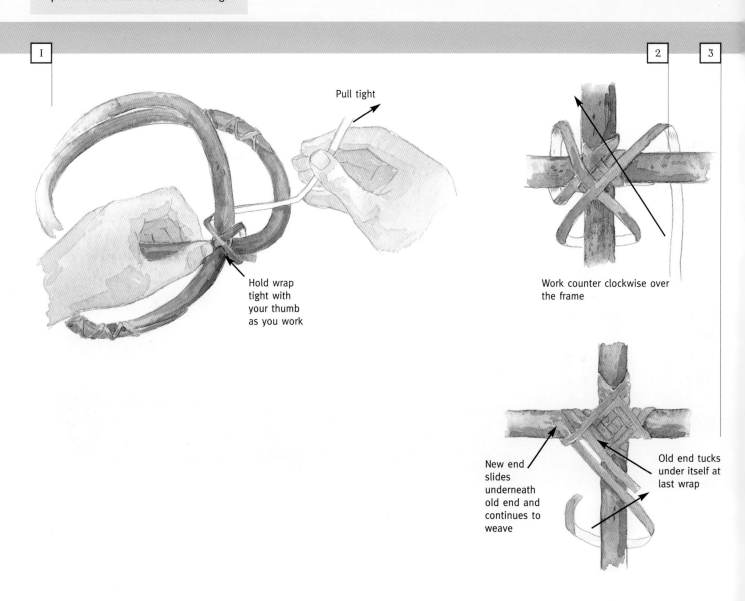

I

Pull tight

Hold wrap tight with your thumb as you work

2 3

Work counter clockwise over the frame

New end slides underneath old end and continues to weave

Old end tucks under itself at last wrap

Cordage

Twisting a section of any soft fiber turns it into something strong and useful. Rope is made from many twisted strands, in which the twist all runs the same way. These are then corded together in the opposite direction. The tension between the twist to the right, and the ply to the left, locks them in place against each other, preventing them from unraveling. Cord can be made by rolling the materials on your thigh and twisting them together or by using the method described here.

Making Rush Cord

1. Prepare a bundle of rushes by dampening and mellowing overnight. Start by overlapping the tip ends of two rushes and tie them to a support. Divide them into two sections and hold them under tension. Twist the bunch in your right hand to the right.

2. Now cross this over to the left on top of the bunch in your left hand. At the same time slide your left hand underneath and to the right. Change hands. Repeat the action. Keep the tension even and the angle constant.

3. **To join:** add a new rush to the group on the right by the butt end, laying it into the "∧"-shape at the center of the gap and twisting to the right. Try not to join ends on both sides in the same place. Keep joining to maintain the width of the cord.

4. Every now and then you will need to straighten the cord. Let go to allow the tension that has built up to unwind slightly. You can trim any ends off very close later with scissors. Using this technique you can make cord of almost any soft material, even short lengths.

The Incas in Peru made aerial rope walkways to cross from one side of mountainous ravines to another. Each villager had a quota of rope to fulfil (rather like a tax), corded from the grass growing there. Many, many yards were then twisted into thick multistranded ropes. These were strung out between the stone buttresses constructed on either side of the walkway, and knotted into a flexible gridlike runner. Two more ropes made the handrails, which were attached to the swinging bridge by vertical strands.

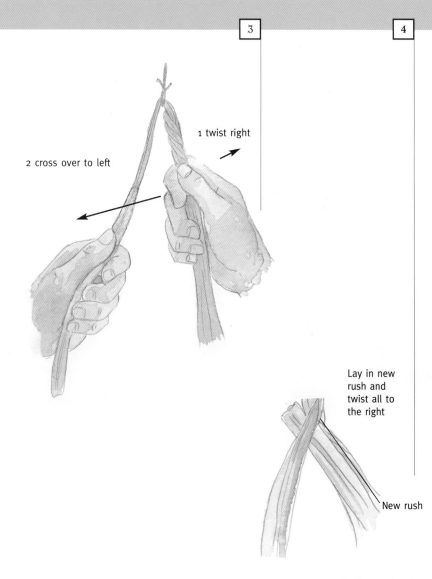

1 twist right

2 cross over to left

Lay in new rush and twist all to the right

New rush

Plaiting

Plaiting (or braiding) can be used to make strips that are narrow or wide, round, flat, or square. Most people will have learned to make the three-strand plait commonly used for braiding hair. This method can be expanded to make a flat plait using odd or even numbers of elements, the more you add the wider the plait. The edges can be folded or twisted to give different effects. It is easier to plait with an uneven number as the turn on both edges will always fold the same way.

Seven-strand Flat Plait

1 Fold seven rushes in half. Lay them flat on a table. Arrange with the folded ends up so that four on the right are crossing three on the left at a diagonal. Weight the ends down. Weave them through each other in a simple over-one, under-one pattern.

2 Always plait with outside rush on the side that has four strands. Fold it across itself and weave over one under one to the opposite side. Repeat this keeping the "^"-shape in the center constant, and pulling the rushes flat.

To join: Lay in a new butt end and overlap for several moves.

3 When finished the plait can be dampened and rolled with a rolling pin to flatten the weave. To sew it together use soft jute garden string. Thread a length of this through a blunt bodkin (or a curved upholstery needle) and catch the outside loops of the plaits alternately, working your way along.

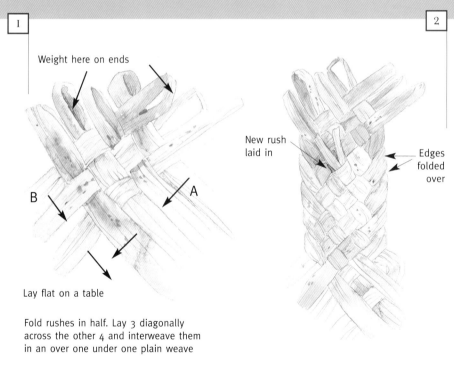

I

Weight here on ends

B   A

Lay flat on a table

Fold rushes in half. Lay 3 diagonally across the other 4 and interweave them in an over one under one plain weave

2

New rush laid in

Edges folded over

3

To sew plaits together

Around the world there are variations of plaits, simple and complex, each suited to its particular function. Ties, wraps, lashings, and slings can all be plaited. Long lengths of flat plait can also be coiled and sewn to make bags, hats, and baskets. The plait in the project Rope-and-Tie Tassels, (shown on page 51) for a pelmet is one in which there are vertical and diagonal elements; the sennit is a series of knots that will make a braid; the Turk's Head, used for the ring, is a three-strand plait worked in a circle.

Seven-strand Straw Plait

Here is a different type of plait – it has a cylindrical spiral form, lending itself to being made around a mold, or freeform in your hand. Always use an odd number of weavers, usually five, seven, or nine, depending on the diameter you want to make.

1 The material you use must be able to make the sharp bends that make the plait, without cracking. You cannot easily make joins in this plait, except in straw, which is tapered and hollow, so either your material has to be in long lengths—cane is suitable—or the plait should cover a short section.

2 Tie the seven strands together tightly at one end, hold in the palm of your hand with the end tucked between your fingers. You can also make this plait with a hollow core by tying the strands around a former; this could be doweling.

3 Arrange six of the strands at even spacings, and kink them down so that they lie out horizontally. The last strand (1) is put in close to (2). Kink them so that they lie out flat. Lift straw 1 over straws 2 and 3, and then lay it down to the far side.

4 Now move straw 3 in the same way over 1 and 4, and lay it down to the far side.

5 Repeat this action, always picking up the straw before the one you have just put down and lifting it over two straws.

6 Increasing and decreasing: To increase, alter the position of the straws a little at a time bringing them back to rest closer to, or just above, the next straw to be worked. To decrease, move the working straw further on to close the gap.

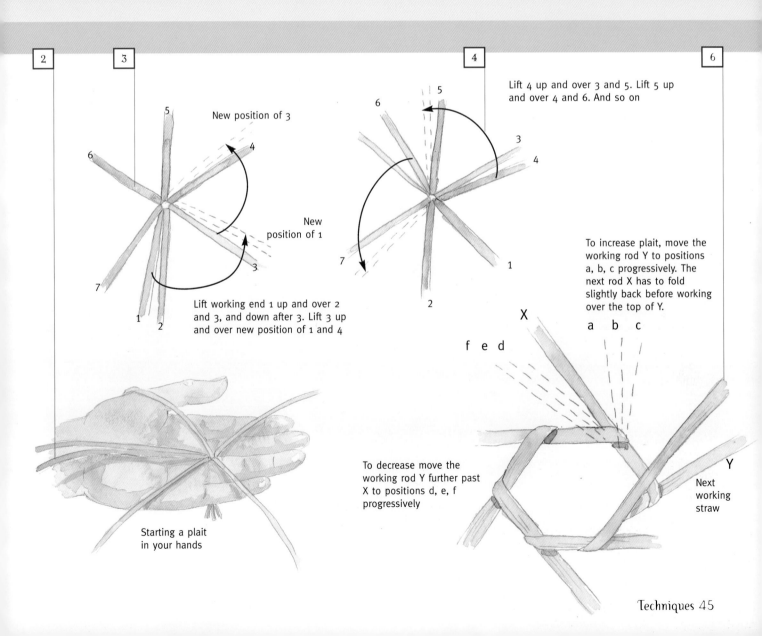

2

3

New position of 3

5

6

4

New position of 1

3

7

1   2

Lift working end 1 up and over 2 and 3, and down after 3. Lift 3 up and over new position of 1 and 4

Starting a plait in your hands

4

Lift 4 up and over 3 and 5. Lift 5 up and over 4 and 6. And so on

5

6

3

4

7

1

2

6

To increase plait, move the working rod Y to positions a, b, c progressively. The next rod X has to fold slightly back before working over the top of Y.

f e d

a   b   c

X

To decrease move the working rod Y further past X to positions d, e, f progressively

Y

Next working straw

Decorative Weaving

Decorative Coils

Decorative coils are easy and fun to make. You can vary the size by using thick or thin doweling and colored cane or dyed willow. Make large coils to stand in a vase or small sizes to decorate your gifts.

You Will Need

- Twenty four 3ft/90cm or 4ft/1.20m colored willow rods for large coils OR colored cane in sizes No. 0 or 5 for smaller coils
- 3ft/90cm length of 1in/2.5cm diameter doweling for larger coils
- 2ft/60cm length of ¾in/2.5cm doweling for smaller coils
- ³⁄₁₆in/50mm and ⅛in/30mm drill bits
- Elastic bands
- Shears/secateurs

1 Make sure the willow or cane has been soaked and mellowed. Drill a series of holes 2in/5cm apart in the larger dowel and 1½in/3.5cm apart in the 2ft/60cm dowel.

2 Starting at the bottom of the dowel, thread the tip end of a willow rod or piece of cane right through the hole, and wind six times tightly around the dowel, cranking the rod as you go to put a twist in it (see Cranking Willow Rods page 40). Kink the end and then bend it down to lie along the dowel and secure the butt with an elastic band. Hold the dowel in your left hand and turn it to the left as you twist up the willow with your right hand.

3 Work up the dowel with the rest of the rods. If you are using cane you do not need to crank it. For small coils, do the same with the tip ends of small rods or No.0 cane on the thinner dowel.

4 Leave to dry thoroughly in a warm place. Remove the coils from the top of the dowel downward. Cut through the tip of each willow rod or piece of cane on either side of the drilled hole. Remove the elastic band and slide the coil off. The coils will look like a tightly coiled spring. When you are ready to use them, pull on the tip end to loosen the coil.

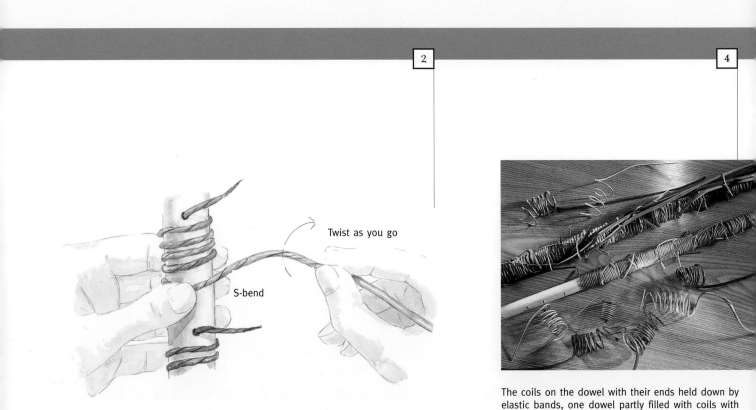

2

Twist as you go

S-bend

4

The coils on the dowel with their ends held down by elastic bands, one dowel partly filled with coils with the drilled holes showing, and the finished coils.

Parcel Wraps

Ply your own cord to tie up a special gift. The bow is twisted into the cord as you work, and you can use your own mixture of grasses and leaves. Here I have used crocosmia leaves, but watsonia or iris are also suitable. The leaves must be long, soft, and fibrous. Collect and completely dry them first, then spray with water from a mister, and keep them wrapped in a damp towel while you work. The oat straw used in this cord gives it a golden sheen. Colored raffia plyed into the cord can be used to give a striped effect to the cord.

You Will Need

- Four rushes
- A handful of oat straw
- A handful of crocosmia leaves
- G-clamps
- Block of wood
- Scissors

1 Have all the materials mellowed. Take one rush, bend it in half, and also bend in half a few of the crocosmia leaves. Add them in to the bend of the rush. Anchor all the materials firmly to a table by clamping them to a block of wood with a G-clamp. Alternatively, tie a piece of strong string around the center and attach to a support, such as table leg. You must be able to put the cord under tension as you make it. Begin to make cord with the two separate bunches (see Making Rush Cord page 43). As you work, keep adding in more material; add the oat straw to the leaves as well. As you work the cord should thicken up.

Aim to have the thickest part of the cord, where you will make the bow, in the center of your parcel. It will look rather untidy at this stage as there will be a lot of loose ends.

2 Make the bow by looping up some of the material from the bunch in your right hand and catching it around your right thumb. Twist the bunch in your right hand over to the left to secure the loop. Do this four times, twice with each bunch.

3 Continue making the cord, letting it get thinner to match the first half. Remove it from the clamp and tidy up with a sharp pair of scissors, pulling on the ends and cutting them off close.

4 To finish the bow, cut through the bottom of the two outside loops and trim off the ends of the material. Split the rush into strands by tearing along the grain.

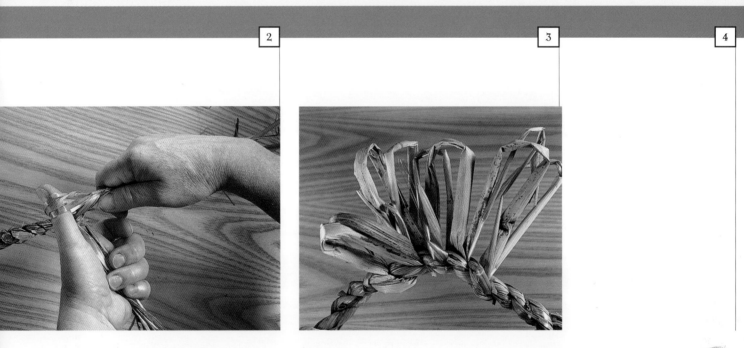

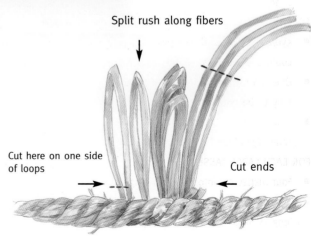

Split rush along fibers

Cut here on one side of loops

Cut ends

Rope-and-Tie Tassels

These fantasy curtain trimmings made from different types of colored cane and soft rush use a mixture of cording, plaiting, and knotting techniques.

You Will Need (for one tie-back):

FOR THE TWO RINGS

- 3ft/90cm blue flatband cane ⁵⁄₁₆in/8mm wide
- 3ft/90cm maroon oval flat cane ³⁄₁₆in/4mm wide

FOR THE SENNIT BRAID

- 5yd/4.5m rush cord (see page 52) or you could use seagrass
- One extra length of rush cord 2ft/60cm long to tie on the tassel
- Two lengths of ⁵⁄₁₆in/8mm wide flatband cane, dyed blue

FOR EACH LARGE TASSEL

- Four rushes cut into 3ft/90cm lengths
- Three pieces each of flat cane 3ft/90cm long in blue and maroon

- Strong cord 18in/45cm long
- One bead approximately ¼in/6mm diameter

FOR THE PELMET PLAIT WITH TASSELS

- Two lengths of chair-seating lapping cane
- Maroon-center cane No. 4
- Green-center cane No. 6, each of these to be slightly longer than the length of the pelmet
- ⁵⁄₁₆in/8mm wide flatband cane in blue and yellow
- One rush for each tassel along the length (one every 5in/12.5cm)

All materials should be well soaked and mellowed

- Sidecutters
- Scissors
- A large-eyed darning needle
- A G-clamp and a small block of wood to anchor the pelmet plait while making it
- Glue or tiny tacks

1 To make the rings – two for each tie-back: The ring is a continuous three-strand plait known as a Turk's-head knot. Take the blue cane with the maroon cane laid on top of it, and wrap it into a double loop 2in/5cm in diameter with the long end on the right. Cross the left loop over the right loop and hold the crossing between your thumb and index finger as in Fig. 1.

2 Taking the loose end, bring it up and over the top of the right-hand loop and thread away through the center to the left under the left loop. It is easier to work first the blue and then the maroon cane.

3 Rotate the ring toward yourself so that the opposite side is facing you. Bring the working end of cane to the top and thread it over the left-hand cane of the ring, into the center and under the right-hand cane of the ring, continuing the plait pattern.

4 Now cross the two original loops of cane over each other, left over right. Take the working cane through the center of these two to complete the pattern.

5 The finishing and starting ends should now meet up. Thread the finishing end over the starting end for two strokes, overlapping them to prevent the ring unraveling (or use glue). When the ring is dry and set in place, cut these off neatly. Make a second ring.

6 **The sennit braid:** Find the center of the rush cord and wrap it around one of the rings. Slip the blue cane under the rush vertically so that it is divided equally in half.

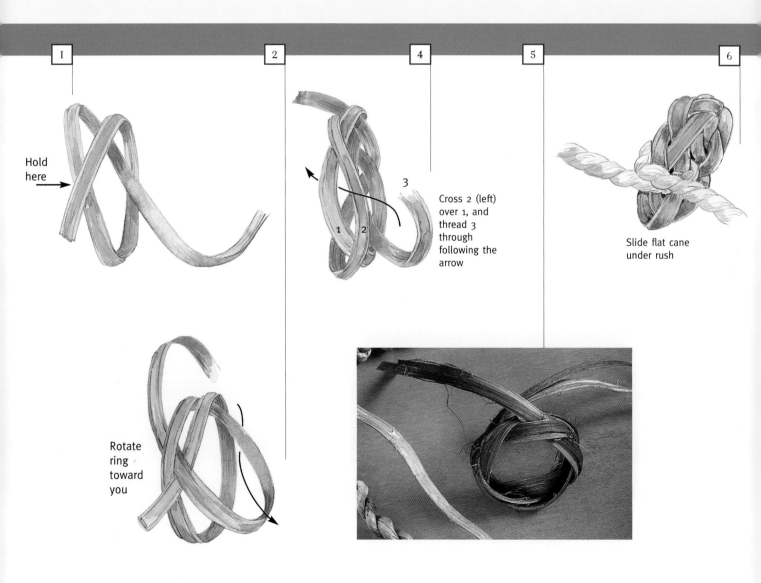

1

Hold here →

Rotate ring toward you

2

3

1 2

4

Cross 2 (left) over 1, and thread 3 through following the arrow

5

6

Slide flat cane under rush

7 Fold the two ends of the cane over and under the rush so that you form a square that looks like this. Working counter-clockwise and starting at 1, fold the rush cord and canes, in order, over to their opposite sides following the numbering. The cane 4, that makes the last move, is threaded under the first cord you folded across.

8 Your sennit will now look like Fig. 8. Repeat the process but this time work clockwise starting with 1, and threading 4 away under 1 at the end. Your sennit will again look like Fig. 7. These two sequences make the sennit. Repeat them over and over again until the braid measures 20in/50cm. If you need to join in the cane at any point, overlap the ends for several moves to secure them.

9 Join the sennit braid to the second ring. Do this by folding the two cane ends back into the braid for a few moves before trimming them off. Cut the two rush cords to 10in/25cm. Now unravel each of them and remake a single cord around the second ring, using one end from each cord. Wrap them around each other following the twist and then thread all four loose ends back into the braid until they are secure. Trim them neatly.

10 **Making the tassel:** The tassel is tied to the sennit braid on a length of corded rush. You can make it onto the cord or over a former—such as a pencil. To start cut 3ft/90cm lengths of rush and flat cane in maroon and blue and fold them over the cord or former. Using the tip end of a rush, twist it to make it stronger and make a tight wrap (see page 40) just below the former.

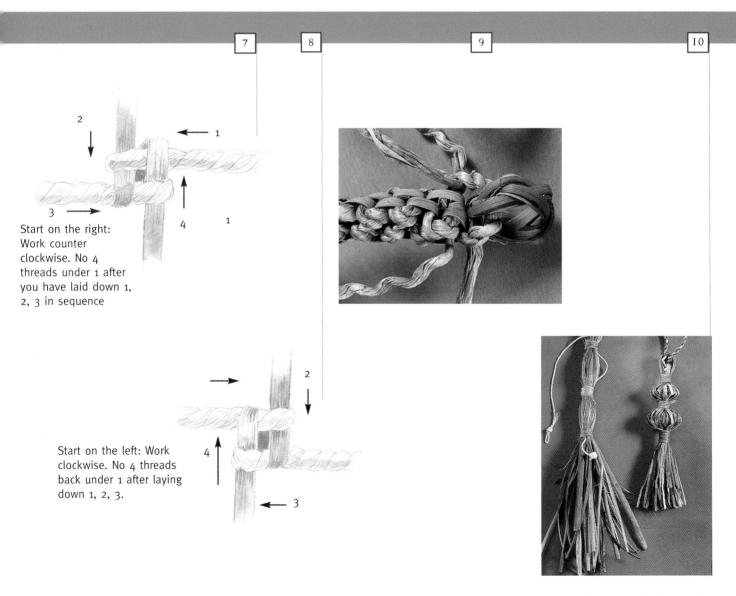

7 | 8 | 9 | 10

Start on the right: Work counter clockwise. No 4 threads under 1 after you have laid down 1, 2, 3 in sequence

Start on the left: Work clockwise. No 4 threads back under 1 after laying down 1, 2, 3.

11 Thread the strong cord through the needle and tie the bead to the other end. Pull the needle up through the wrap so that the bead will be hidden in the center of the bunch, and so that it will be below the level of the third wrap.

12 Now shred the rush-and-cane skirt into finer strips, so that it will be softer to pull up to make the tassel.

13 Make another two tight wraps at B and C. Before pulling up the tassel, hold between both fists and roll them around to soften the fibers.

14 Pull on the string to bring the bead up to the bottom tie, and push the rush and cane into two loops. Sew away the cord into the top of the tassel so that it is held tight. Trim the skirt level with scissors. Attach to the sennit with a rush-cord tie.

15 The pelmet plait: Lay the lapping cane and green and maroon center cane out flat, and the blue and yellow flatband cane at diagonals, and anchor under the wood block with the G-clamp. The flatband must be well soaked and mellowed so it does not split. Make sure you are folding on the smooth side of the cane (see page 14).

16 The flatband canes fold diagonally across the vertical canes. Fold first the yellow and then the blue cane. Be sure to follow the diagram carefully. The folds in this stage lock against the vertical canes making a wide plait. In the second stage of the plait, the folds wrap close to the vertical canes. This gives the plait a serrated edge. The tassels will fit neatly into these flat spaces and the serrations prevent them slipping along the plait.

17 Fold first the yellow, then the blue cane following the diagram. If you need to join the flatband cane overlap the new and old ends for a few movements.

18 To make simple tassels with rush, fold a few lengths over the plait at regular intervals, make a wrap, and shred and trim the skirt. Attach to the pelmet with glue or tiny tacks.

19 Varnish all the sections lightly to bring out the color and prevent them collecting dust.

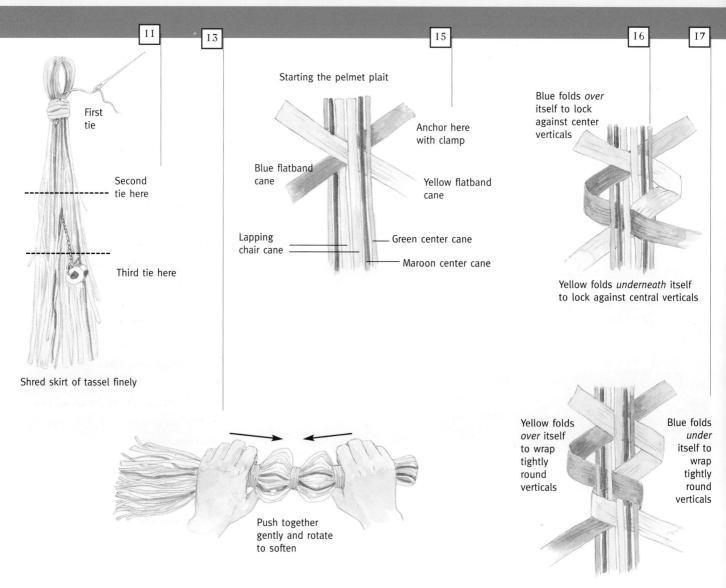

11 **13**

First tie

Second tie here

Third tie here

Shred skirt of tassel finely

Push together gently and rotate to soften

15 Starting the pelmet plait

Anchor here with clamp

Blue flatband cane

Yellow flatband cane

Lapping chair cane

Green center cane

Maroon center cane

16 Blue folds *over* itself to lock against center verticals

Yellow folds *underneath* itself to lock against central verticals

17

Yellow folds *over* itself to wrap tightly round verticals

Blue folds *under* itself to wrap tightly round verticals

Harvest Ring

All sorts of soft materials gathered as they ripen, and then dried, can be used to make this ring. Leaves and grasses, or sedges would be suitable; corn and oats give it a golden sheen.

The ring can be hung on a door as a wreath or used as a centerpiece for a table decoration with spiked metal candle holders pushed firmly into the plait; be careful not to leave lighted candles unattended.

You Will Need

- Several large handfuls of mixed grasses with ears or seed heads left on (I used rye, oat, and wheat straw)
- Rushes or long reeds—a handful
- 4yd/3.5m of seagrass or any strong natural cord
- If the ring is to hang up—use two lengths of bark for the bow, 2ft/60cm and 4ft/1.2m long ¾in/2.5cm wide. You could use any decorative string—a strip long enough to make a bow.
  All materials should be dampened and mellowed
- Shears/secateurs
- Scissors
- String
- A nail
- A bodkin (or rush threader)
- A plank of wood

1 The ring is made in a four-strand plait which is curved round into a ring when it is long enough. Hammer a nail into an old plank of wood, and tie a piece of thin, but strong string to the nail to attach the materials to, leaving your hands free. Work with the plank between your knees so that you can pull the plait tight.

2 Take a handful of assorted grasses arranged so that there are seedheads at each end. Add to these two rushes, which are laid in so that equal lengths are on each side. Tie the string tightly around them in the center.

3 Lay a similar bunch on top of the first bunch, at right angles. Include the length of seagrass cord in this bundle placing it so that an equal length lies on each side.

4 Holding the center down so that it does not slip, pick up a bunch from underneath. Twist it tightly and bring it up and over the top layer, and then lay it down on the opposite side. Pick up and twist the second bundle from underneath and cross it over in the opposite direction. The bunches should remain at right angles to each other.

5 Since the grasses are short you need to add more material to the core after each crossing. Try to keep the diameter of the core even. Lay another handful of grasses immediately on top of the twisted grass crossing you have just made so that equal lengths stick out either side. (These loose materials will be held in by the next move you make.)

6 Now take a bunch that is from underneath and twist and bring it up and over to the opposite side as you did before. Do this with the second bunch lying underneath.

7 Lay more material flat on top as before. These two movements step 4 and step 6 form the plait, and are repeated until the plait is 34in/86cm long. Add more materials after each move to maintain the thickness of the core and also add a few rushes when the first ones begin to thin out, to strengthen the grasses. Finish the plait so that step 4 is the last movement you make (the bunches without the seagrass in them). The whole plait will look untidy as you work with the ends of the grasses sticking out. Don't worry, they can be trimmed later. Keep a tight twist and tension on the bunches as you work so that you do not lose your place.

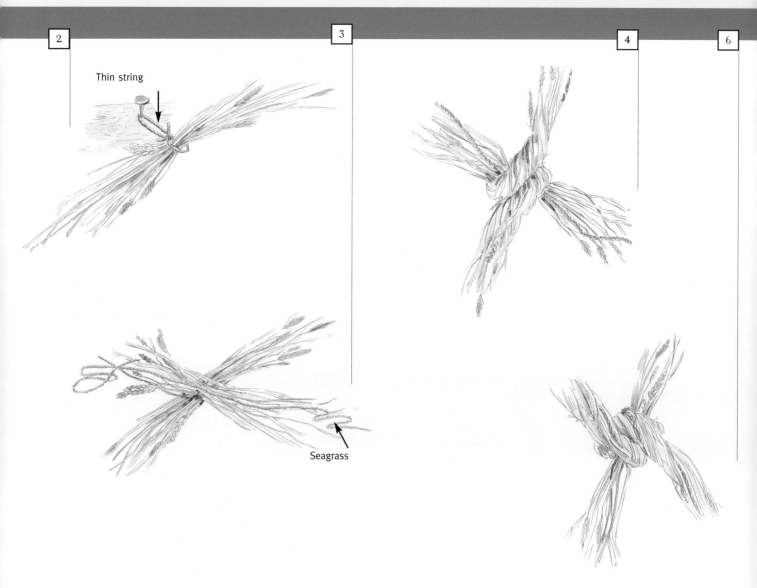

2

Thin string

3

Seagrass

4

6

8 Untie the string holding the plait down. Carefully form the plait into a ring, damping it to make it pliable if it has dried out. Find the seagrass cord and bring it up and through the beginning loop of grasses to replace the string tie. Wrap the seagrass around two ends of the plait twice and pull it tight to bring them together in a seamless ring. Tie the two ends of the seagrass tightly together with a double knot.

9 The two bunches of grasses and rush that belonged with the seagrass now have to be twisted up and threaded away following it. Smaller amounts of any remaining bunches are twisted and threaded away into the plait following the pattern to hide the ends. You can use a bodkin, a rush threader, or the handle end of a wooden spoon to help you push or pull them through the plait.

10 Trim all the loose ends with scissors or shears, but leave the grass seedheads on for their decorative effect.

Making the Bow and Tie

If you wish to hang the ring up you can make a bow using bark which has been soaked and mellowed to soften it.

1 Using the longer and wider strip of bark fold it following the diagram.

2 Cut splits in the second piece of bark as shown. To make the tie wrap the bark around the folded bow threading end A through the split in the center. Now wrap ends A and B right around the plaited ring and tie, A around B, making a knot in the two ends. C is knotted to form a loop for hanging the ring up.

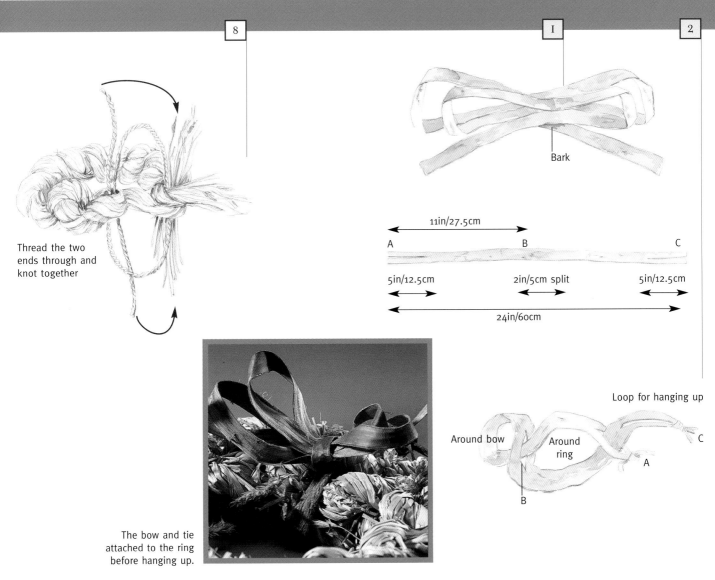

8

Thread the two ends through and knot together

The bow and tie attached to the ring before hanging up.

1

Bark

2

11in/27.5cm

A   B   C

5in/12.5cm   2in/5cm split   5in/12.5cm

24in/60cm

Loop for hanging up

Around bow   Around ring   C

B   A

Gallery

LEFT: These delicate grass bracelets were made by children in Africa. Each plait has a descriptive name that relates to the shape the weave makes.

ABOVE: Coiled hat from Watsonia leaves sewn with heavy cotton twine. *Sally Roadknight.*

ABOVE: Jewel box in exceptionally fine rushwork. Twill weave and diagonal plaiting The handle and loops for closing are corded rush. *Olivia Elton-Barratt.*

ABOVE and LEFT: Basketry sculpture **Please Play for Me**— Sheath base of a long frond from the Cocos Palm. Detail shows the wattle seed pod ties. *Betty Roach.*

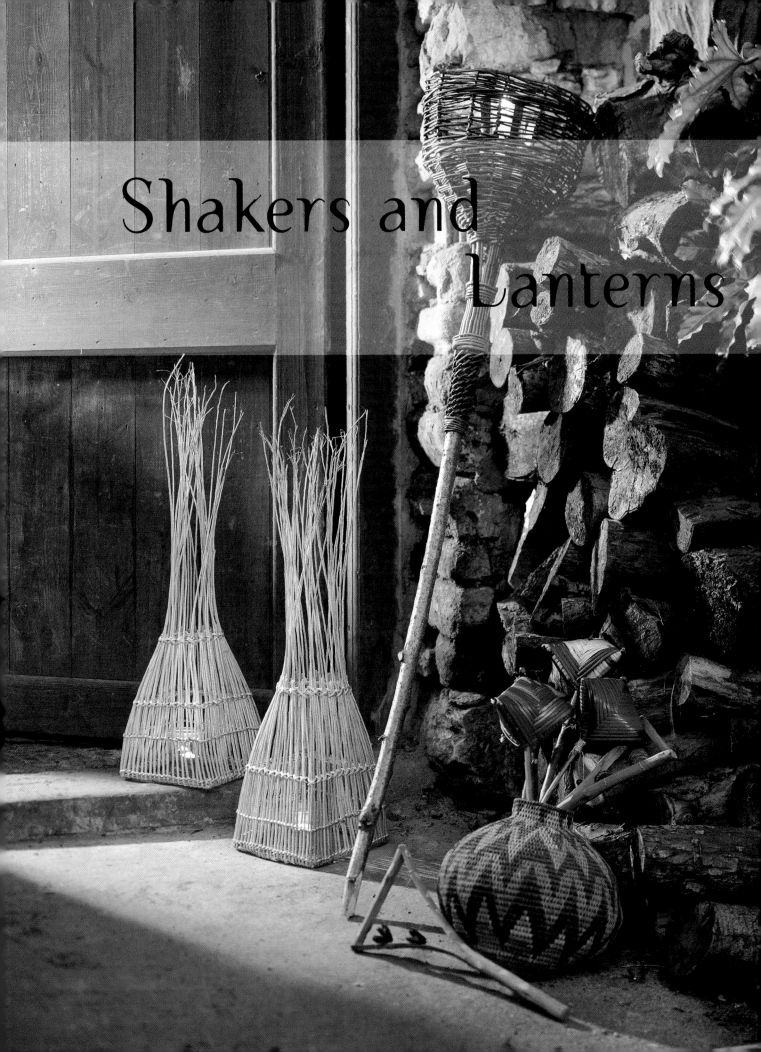

Shakers and Lanterns

Stick Shaker

This shaker is a real musical instrument which is based on a traditional African design. I make these to use in a samba band. In order to get the right sound from the bottle tops, you will need to burn out any plastic inserts, which I do by putting them into a bonfire outside—because of the fumes they give off—and retrieving them when they are cold. This also gives them a satisfying aged look.

You Will Need

- One 18in/45cm length of straight heavy stick ¾in/2cm in diameter, cut green, hazel is ideal
- One 8in/20cm length of similar stick but smaller in diameter to match the thinner end of the first
- Fine galvanized wire
- Ten bottle tops, or you could use circles cut from tin cans with snips
- Two wire nails
- String
- A vise or clamp and workbench to hold the stick while you work
- Small saw
- Small drill and fine bit
- A 1in/2.5cm wide chisel for scraping, and a ¼in/0.5cm chisel for cutting the center
- A hammer
- A fine awl
- Pliers
- Acrylic paint or wood stain to color the shaker
- A small piece of sponge from which to cut shapes for stamped decoration

Project by LYN EDWARDS

1 Anchor the larger stick in the vise and with the *side* of the chisel, not the cutting end, scrape off the bark.

2 Mark the stick at 8in/20cm from the butt end.

3 At the thinner end mark two parallel lines ¼in/0.5cm apart, from the top down to the mark. Saw carefully down along these. Do this a section at a time along each line, working both cuts progressively along at the same time. At the mark use the narrow chisel to cut away the center of the stick.

4 Turn the large stick on its side and clamp it steady. Drill three holes right through both sections at ⅓in/1cm, 2½in/6.5cm, and 4½in/11.5cm starting from the top.

5 Wrap a length of string several times around the stick, just below the sawn part, and tie it tightly.
This will prevent the split running down the stick when you insert the top wedge. Shave the bark off the smaller stick and cut to shape and dimensions shown. Gently wedge the smaller stick in place at the top end and pin through the top holes with the wire nails.

6 Hammer the bottle tops flat. Holding them on a flat surface, pierce down through the center with the awl. Thread them onto two lengths of the galvanized wire, six on the top and four on the bottom, and secure through the holes as shown using the pliers to twist the ends around.

7 Untie the string. Stain or paint the shaker, and when it is dry decorate it with simple stamped designs cut from the sponge.

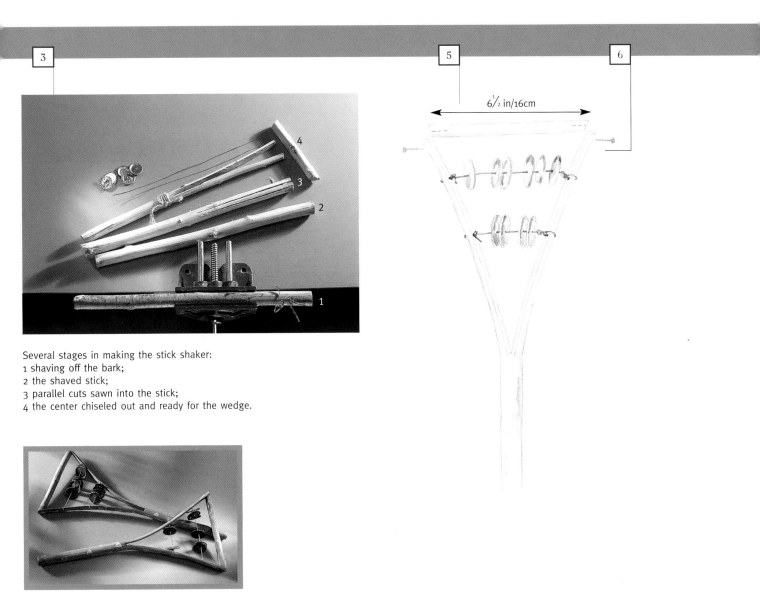

6½in/16cm

Several stages in making the stick shaker:
1 shaving off the bark;
2 the shaved stick;
3 parallel cuts sawn into the stick;
4 the center chiseled out and ready for the wedge.

Pyramidal Shaker

The first time I came across the ideal shape for a three-dimensional "god's eye" was on an antique Chinese jacket, where minute diamonds were made in fine gold thread, which in this context hung from the hem as a decoration. It took a while to work out how to make them, but once started, the pattern is easy to follow.

Project by LYN EDWARDS

You Will Need

- Thick card 12in/30cm x 4in/10cm
- A strong stick 16in/40cm long
- Masking tape
- Dried peas
- Multipurpose glue
- Strong thread
- One large wooden bead, three smaller ones
- 106in/270cm flat oval lapping cane dyed red, and 300in/762cm turquoise flat oval lapping cane, soaked and mellowed

(If you plan to use your own color scheme, six long lengths of dyed cane will be enough to wrap one shaker)
- A sharp knife
- A ruler
- Pencil
- A long needle, minimum 8in/20cm long (an upholstery needle is ideal)
- Varnish

1 **Making the former:** Trace the following design onto paper and then enlarge to 12 x 4in/30 x 10cm. Trace onto the card, make the points A to H and cut out.

2 Score along all dotted lines so they can be folded. Cut the notches where indicated to accommodate the stick: a small notch at point C (top), a slightly larger notch at point F (bottom). Angle the corner at points A and H.

3 To form the six-sided shape, bring F to H and D to E. Tape across the short sides E/D to H/F.

4 Sharpen the thinner end of the stick like a pencil and insert through the lower notch F/H until the sharpened end protrudes just beyond the top notch A/C. Holding it upright, drop in a few dried peas and tape across the other two short sides A/C to B and A/C to D/E.

5 Apply a little glue at both the top and bottom notches to prevent the stick from twisting, and then glue the large wooden bead firmly onto the sharpened end, making sure it is in contact with the card former.

6 **To start the weaving:** Hold the shaker upright, tape the short end of the cane to the short edge B to A/C with the long end facing the top. A dab of glue on the underside of the three points will help to stop the cane from slipping.

7 Start weaving by bringing the cane up to the top A/C, down to point D/E, back to the top A/C, down to point G, back to the top, down to point B, then back to the top.

8 Continue in this way ensuring that the weaving material sits neatly side by side and does not overlap. Once you have started it is easy to follow the pattern. This shaker has 3 rows turquoise, 3 rows red, 3 rows turquoise, 2 rows red, 3 rows turquoise. You can design your own pattern. As long as you remember always to come back to the top after each weave you will find that you cannot go wrong.

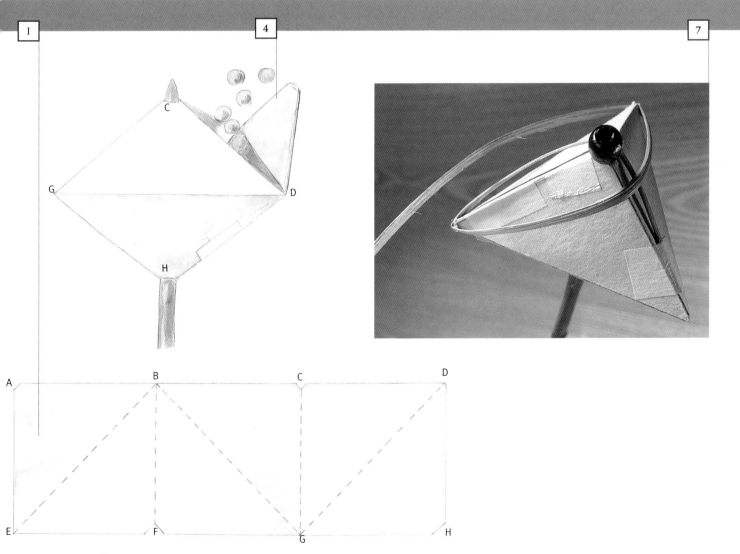

Enlarge to 12 x 4in/30 x 10cm

9 To join in additional lengths and when you change color, cut and tape them onto the underside of the shaker, as this will be covered by successive rows of weaving.

10 When you have covered all the card former, finish off by threading the end away into the weave and gluing it in place.

11 To add the small beads to the edges, thread lengths of the string from points G to B, B to E/D, and E/D to G, leaving ends at each of the three points. Tie on the beads and knot securely.

12 Finish off the shaker by applying a coat of varnish to the cane.

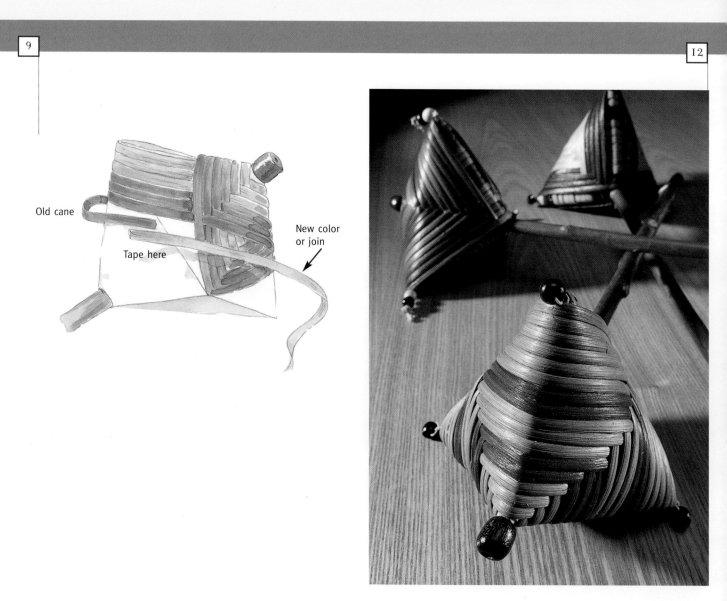

9

Old cane

Tape here

New color or join

12

Sentinel Lantern

Inspiration for this lantern came from a Chinese bamboo candleholder for the garden. The main stick is split at the top to hold a night light in a glass jar. The light shines through the zig zag openwork weave of the shade creating flickering patterns. Several following a path make a procession to light the way. The lantern is for use outside in a safe position. It is most easily made if the stick is firmly driven into the ground once the top section has been split into four. Alternatively, a length of metal piping—slightly larger than the end of the stick—sunk into the ground will make a permanent site. You can then swivel it inside the piping and sit underneath to do the weaving. This also makes it easy to remove when you are not using it.

You Will Need

- A freshly cut stick 1¼ in/3cm diameter at the butt end and 5ft/1.5m long (I used hazel, but any straight, stout gathered material that will split is suitable)
- Sixteen 5ft/1.5m willow rods
- A small bundle of 4ft/1.2m willow, some slender, some thicker
- Four thicker rods to make the wedge (short sticks)
- String
- Tape
- A small glass jar to hold the night light
- A pruning saw (to cut down the stick)
- A heavy blunt knife for splitting for stick
- A mallet or hammer
- A vise or workbench
- A knife
- A bodkin
- Shears/secateurs

1 **Splitting the stick and starting the weaving:** Measure 14in/35.5cm from the top (narrow end) of the stick and wrap a length of string several times around at this point and tie tightly. This will prevent the stick from splitting the rest of the way down its length. Clamp it firmly in a workbench or vise so that you can work on this end.

2 Using a heavy blunt knife (you do not need a sharp blade since it is not a cutting edge), drive it in, using the mallet, across the center of the grain. Split down to the string. Split again to make quarters, (see Splitting Materials page 34). If you are working outside, shave the bottom end of the stick to a point and drive it well into the ground. Otherwise, clamp it upright in a way that will make it comfortable to work on.

3 Wedge two to four short thick sticks into the splits to open them up.

4 Shave away some of the pith wood and smooth any splinters.

5 Take the 5ft/1.5m rods. Use a willow wrap (see Wrapping page 40) to tie them, four to each quarter, covering the string. Leave 5in/12.5cm of the butt ends sticking out below the wrap.

6 Now work several rows of pairing (see Pairing page 24) to secure the uprights to the split sticks and then open them out to form the lantern shape. Do this by pushing the butt ends of two 4ft/1.2m rods into two consecutive splits, and working two rows of pairing over the stick and willows. Now kink the willow uprights out almost horizontally, and, dividing them into sets of two, pair over them for three rows. Then divide and pair over them singly. Join with more weavers tip to tip and butt to butt (page 24) and end the band of pairing with tips.

7 **Slewing:** Now begin a section of three-rod slewing (see Slewing page 29). Work two sets chasing each other. Use the smallest weavers in your bundle. If you find slewing difficult to do you can continue pairing instead. Continue weaving until you have a diameter of 11in/28cm.

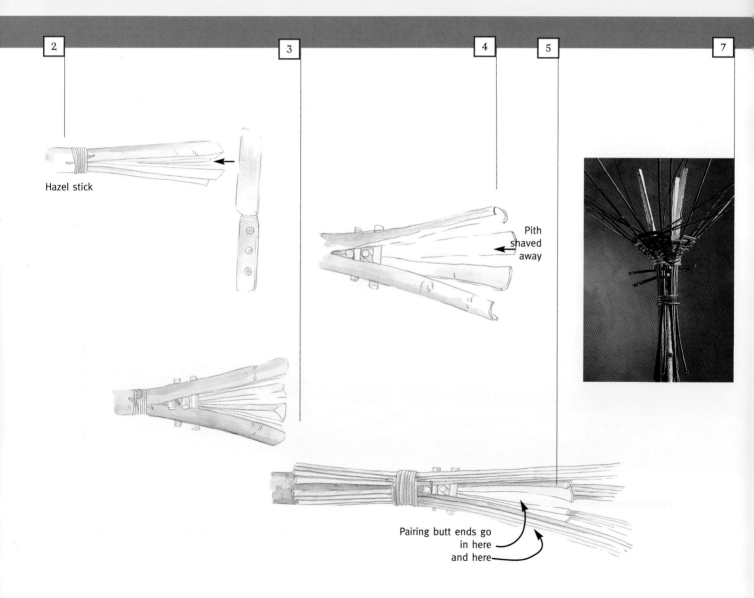

Hazel stick

Pith shaved away

Pairing butt ends go in here and here

8 **Waling:** Kink the stakes vertically upright now and weave a band of waling (see Waling page 28) to keep them in place. Use 4in/1.2m weavers. Begin with three tips, and work out to butts and then back to tips. You should have at least two rows. Push the stakes up so that they are almost vertical as you weave.

9 **Zig zag weave:** Sort out 18 more 4ft/1.2m weavers for the zig zag weave (see Zig Zag weave page 31). Use one weaver to each space, starting with the butt ends. Weave them backward and forward over the stakes, out to the tips.

10 Another set of waling is worked above this to make a firm base for the border. Use two sets of three weavers, starting and ending with the tips.

11 **The border:** This is a trac (see Trac Borders page 32). Each stake kinks to the right and works, in front of one, then behind one, for the next eight stakes. Each stake ends inside the lantern and is left there to be trimmed later. To set the correct height of the border kink the first eight stakes 1in/2.5cm above the waling, by bending them to the right at that point.

12 **Seven-straw plait handle decoration:** Arrange seven 4ft/1.2m rods around the post, 10in/25.5cm below the string tie, butt ends up and make a wrap around the tip ends. Kink them out horizontally and then plait up the stick until you reach the butt ends of the tied uprights. Slot the butts of the plait weavers in between these ends and make a wrap over both. Cut off any ends showing above the wrap.

13 **Holding in the night-light jar:** The four parts of the split stick hold the jar. Push the jar between them. Around the top, pair two rods, with a double twist in the gaps (see diagram 7 of Conical Plant Support project on page 111), so that the jar cannot fall out. Push the ends of the pairing under the weave.

14 Trim all ends neatly.

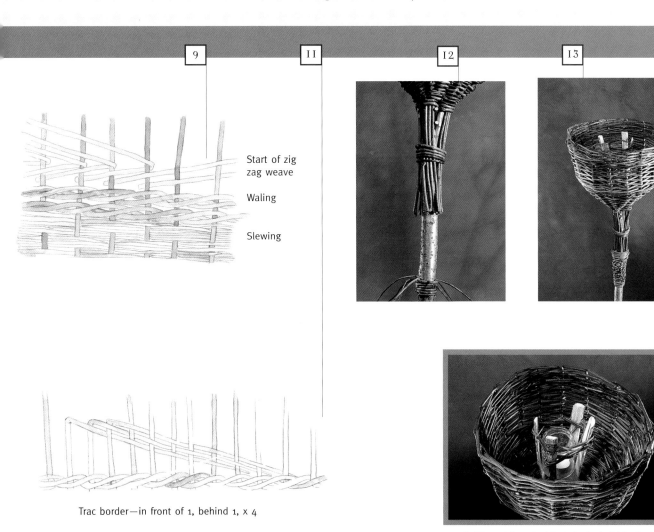

9

Start of zig zag weave

Waling

Slewing

Trac border—in front of 1, behind 1, x 4

11

12

13

Pairing with a double twist to hold in the jar

White Willow Lantern

Using fine white willow you can create this delicate, bottomless lantern. Place it on a table, over a candle or night light in a glass jar, and the weave will be illuminated. Experience in scalloming and fitching, both techniques requiring skill and attention to detail, is helpful in following this project. Do not leave the lantern unattended if you are using it with a candle or night light; this lantern should be used by adults only.

You Will Need

- Two x 6ft/1.8m stout white willow rods $^3/_8$in/1cm at the butt end, soaked and mellowed (ideally one should be marginally thicker than the other)
- 26ft/8.2cm skeined white willow, $^3/_8$in/1cm wide (see Making Skeins page 34) OR you may use No. 5 split cane (dip them in water and wrap them in a damp towel)
- Approximately 88 well-matched 3ft/90cm white willow rods, soaked and mellowed
- 4 x 3ft willow rods, for the fitching
- A piece of flat scrap wood at least 9 x 9in/22.5 x 22.5cm
- 10 headless nails
- A sharp knife
- Shears/secateurs
- A hammer
- A pencil and ruler
- A damp towel

1 **Making the frames:** On the piece of wood mark out a square 7½ x 7½in/19 x 19cm. Inside this, mark out another square 6 x 6in/15 x 15cm. Hammer eight nails some way into the corners and two more nails at positions A and B, slightly outside the line of the squares as shown in Fig. 1.

2 Brace the butt end of the 6ft/1.8m rod against the inside of B and make a frame by bending it around the square of nails. Overlap the ends by 5in/12.5cm and cut off the tip. Keep the butt end on the outside for strength. Make the second frame starting at point A using the butt end of the slightly thinner second willow rod. Overlap the join by 3in/7.5cm as in Fig. 2. For detailed instructions for making hoops and shaped frames see page 38.

3 Make a 4in/10cm diameter hoop from the remaining piece of the second rod. Shave the butts and tips of these three frames and lash together with cane or fine willow from the 26ft/8m skein as in Fig. 3 (see page 39).

4 **Scalloming the stakes onto the frame:** Cut 8in/20cm scalloms on the butt ends of the 3ft/90cm rods (see page 36), using scalloming to start the weaving. Scallom them onto the largest frame starting in the center of the side opposite the join in the frame, and work to the left. They must be very close together. The number of rods you need will vary slightly according to the diameter of the rods you select. You should get close to 22 on each side. On the corners cut away some of the excess tails of the scalloms to make a neat shape and place one scallom right on the corner. Arrange them so that you have an even number on each side plus one on each corner. When you reach the beginning again, cut off the remaining scallom tails and weave the tail of the final scallom away between the beginning rods.

5 **Fitching:** Using a pencil, mark lightly across the stakes 3in/7.5cm up from the base frame. Begin fitching at this height on the opposite side of the lantern to the end of the scalloming. Use a pair of fine matched 3ft/90cm rods. Follow the instructions for fitching on page 26.

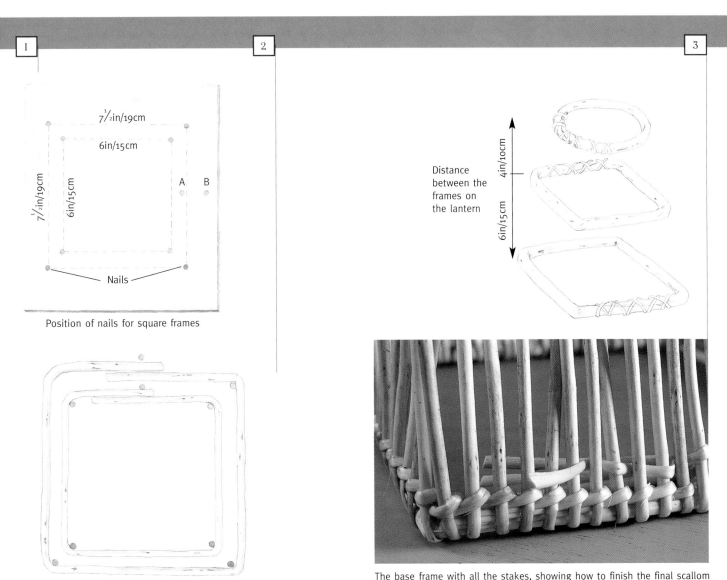

1

7½in/19cm

6in/15cm

7½in/19cm

6in/15cm

A   B

Nails

Position of nails for square frames

Making the frames

2

3

4in/10cm

Distance between the frames on the lantern

6in/15cm

The base frame with all the stakes, showing how to finish the final scallom

6 You will need to make a join half way round the lantern. Use the second pair of fine rods and join butts to butts. Make the join to the right of the center on this side, but before you reach the corner. Do not make the joins in two consecutive spaces as it will be impossible to get the stakes to lie close together. Pull very tightly on the new fitching rod as you join, and push the stake hard to the left to keep the gap even. Work around to the beginning and overlap the start of the fitching by several strokes.

7 Finish the fitching by threading the tip ends of the rod down through consecutive fitches in the lower row, using a bodkin to open up a space. Pull the weaving rods tight and cut off the ends leaving ⅛in/.25cm to prevent the joins slipping. Each side should measure 7in/8cm at this point.

8 **Adding the second and third frames:** Lightly mark the stakes at 6in/15cm above the base frame. Place the second square frame inside the lantern. Using split cane or the willow skein, lash the stakes in pairs, following Fig. 8, working three stakes together on the corners. Secure the ends and any joins under the lashing.

9 Tie the tips in a bunch while you lash the final hoop inside. Mark the stakes with a pencil at 10in/25.5cm from the base frame. Place the hoop inside and lash as before, this time working four stakes together at a time. Split up every other one of the previous pairs for a decorative effect.

10 Untie the top and gently curve the tips of the stakes outward. Trim off two out of each group of four stakes just above the top hoop. Untie the top and gently curve the tips of the remaining stakes outward. Leave to dry, keeping in place with a former if necessary. (A small round bowl, lightly wedged in place, works well.)

7

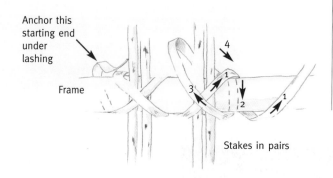

Fitching showing the join

Anchor this starting end under lashing

Frame

Stakes in pairs

How to make the cross lashing

8

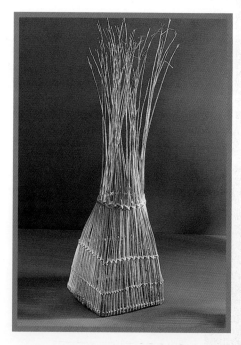

The finished project with its parallel bands of fitching and decorative crossed lashing.

RIGHT: Brown willow fitched eel traps. A traditional French design; a double layer of fitched rods forms a narrowing cone on the inside of the trap into which the eel swims. *Eva Siedenfeld.*

LEFT: Basket made in a square knotting technique. Palm (*Cordyline*). *Hilary Burns.*

ABOVE: Ammonites woven in willow bark (right) and New Zealand flax (left) using straw plait techniques. *Molly Rathbone.*
RIGHT: Colored cane rattle using a straw plait technique. *Hilary Burns.*

Baskets

Egg Basket

Candy stripes and an unusual double handle with a decorative lapped finish make a colorful feature of this frame basket. The hoops and ribs for frame baskets need to be carefully made and measured. Once in place, the shape cannot be adjusted easily. Read the general instructions for frames on page 38.

You Will Need

- Seven or eight large rods ½in/1.5cm diameter at the butt end, at least 6–7ft/1.8–2.1m long. Use the butt ends of the thickest rods to make the handle hoops and top frames, and the remainder to make the ribs
- Flat oval cane, ⅛/4mm width, dyed in the following rather muted colors:
  Four long lengths stone yellow, two navy blue, four pale red, four pale turquoise, two dark green, two pale yellow
- Flatband cane, ¼in/8mm width, in the following colors:
  Two lengths navy blue, two maroon, two turquoise

- Four ¾in/2cm round wire nails
Follow this sequence of colors and sizes when weaving:
- 2ft/60cm each of 4mm flat oval cane navy blue and 8mm maroon for weaving the handle lapping. All materials should be soaked, mellowed, and wrapped in a damp towel
- Shears/secateurs
- A bodkin
- A sharp knife
- A hammer
- Sidecutters or branch cutter

1 **Making the hoop and top frame:**
Prepare the frames for the handle and top rim first. The willow for them must be well mellowed, or you can use semigreen material. If you can make these in advance and allow them to dry in shape you will find it much easier to keep the shape of the basket, but it is not essential. There should be no kinks in the hoops.

2 Make the handle hoops (you will need two exactly the same) by twisting a stout rod (at least 44in/1.1m long) into a loose knot, using up the butt end and pulling on the tip end until you have the right shape. Pin in place with the wire nails, driving them through from the inside at an angle. Cut off any excess rod at an angle.

3 Make the two hoops for the top rim; they are identical and the ends fit inside each other with the butt ends on the outside. Cut one to length and then cut the second exactly the same shape. Shave carefully as shown. They must have a substantial overlap and fit together well.

4 Place the rim hoops inside the handle hoops making sure they are above the halfway mark so that the basket will have depth to it.

5 Weaving the god's eye: Starting with the stone yellow cane weave a god's eye on each side to join the handle hoops to the top frames. Follow instructions on page 42.

6 Adding the ribs: Cut eight lengths of willow from the thick rods for the pairs of ribs. Cut 20in/50cm lengths for the shortest pair (next to the top frame) to allow for shaving down, and 17in/44cm lengths for the shortest pair (next to the handle hoops). Shape these by careful bending and shave the ends of the rods to a point. Place these in the frame first and then judge the lengths of the other two pairs to fit between them. Alternate the tips and butts. This will then even up the sizes and stresses in the basket.

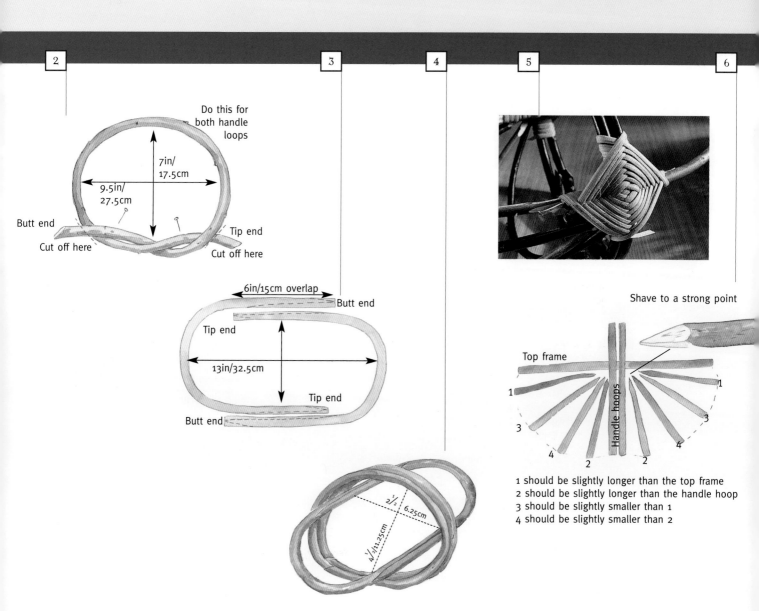

Do this for both handle loops

7in/17.5cm

9.5in/27.5cm

Butt end
Cut off here
Tip end
Cut off here

6in/15cm overlap
Butt end
Tip end
13in/32.5cm
Tip end
Butt end

2½/6.25cm
4½/11.25cm

Shave to a strong point

Top frame

Handle hoops

1 should be slightly longer than the top frame
2 should be slightly longer than the handle hoop
3 should be slightly smaller than 1
4 should be slightly smaller than 2

7 Weaving the body of the basket: Divide the oval flatband cane and wide flatband cane into two bundles with equal amounts of color in each group. Use these to weave the two sides of the basket so that the stripes of color are symmetrical. Begin a randing weave with the navy-blue flat oval cane. For three rows work the ribs in pairs so that you do not have a bulky start. After this split the pairs into singles. Do this from the center to the edge each time in order to have the least visible disruption of the weave. Wrap twice around the handle bow every time to increase the distance you travel along the top frame. The weave always pulls down on the top frame making it dip and look "sad." Keep the frame well pulled up at the two ends.

8 In order always to have the right side of the cane to the outside, and so that you have a smooth surface where it wraps the frame, twist the cane once as you reach the top.

9 Join on with the next color, overlapping by two or more strokes. You should trim so that the cane is cut just where it curves up. When you run your hands over the basket it should have a smooth finish.

10 Weave both sides up evenly, so that you do not unbalance the basket. Be sure to start the weave on both sides in exactly the same way (symmetrically) so that the last row of the basket will meet up.

HINT
The basket will tend to pull outward, because of the tension exerted by the ends of the ribs; you should push down on the long sides (on the god's eye) to keep it in shape. Constantly adjust and be aware of the balance. Make sure the basket sits firm and level on the ribs marked 2. Work on the outside with the basket upside-down over your knee.

11 When you have used up all the oval cane colors, start on the wider cane. Shave the first 4in/10cm about ⅛in/4mm so that there is a smooth join where the thick cane meets the thin cane. At this stage, as you weave the bottom curve of the basket, occasionally make a turn right around the central double hoop. This will prevent the weaving slipping along.

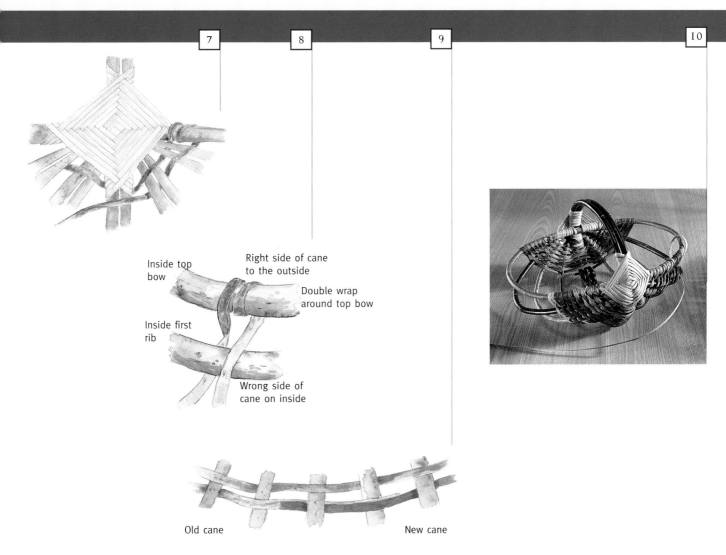

Inside top bow

Right side of cane to the outside

Double wrap around top bow

Inside first rib

Wrong side of cane on inside

Old cane

New cane

12 You will find that you have to use packing (see page 23) to even up the shape. Missing the top frame, work back and forward over the ribs to even up the central space. You should aim to have a straight narrow gap at the end. The last rows on either side of the gap should meet in the middle and overlap in a seamless weave.

13 **To make the handle lapping:** The two lengths of cane work over each other. Start in the middle and wrap long end B over and under short end A for eight turns. Finish by tucking the ends away up into the wrap using a bodkin. Then complete the other side in the same way.

14 Trim and tidy all the ends, then varnish the cane.

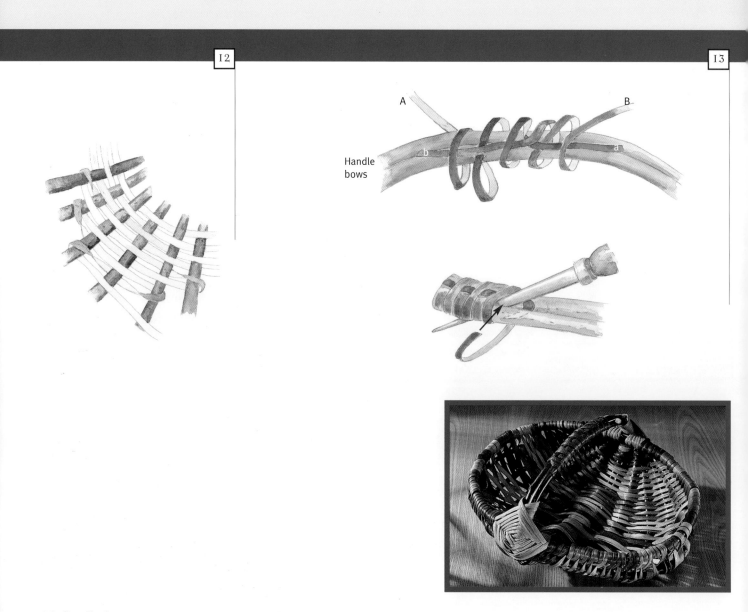

12

13

A

B

Handle
bows

b

a

Frame Basket

Frame baskets are constructed using hoops, ribs, and weavers. They are particularly rustic in style. This melon-shaped basket is made using bark and brown and white willow, and has a twisted cross handle.

You Will Need

- Ten or twelve large rods for hoops and ribs, diameter of ½in/1.5cm at butt end
- Two thick 6/1.8m white willow rods for the handle, one slightly heavier than the other
- A bundle of 5ft/1.5m mixed rods, brown and white for the weaving
- Fine nonstretch cord or skeins for lashing the hoops together
- Bark skein or lapping cane for the god's eye weave
- A sharp knife
- Shears/secateurs
- A fine bodkin

1 Body of the basket: Start by making the hoop frames and cutting out the material for the ribs. You can do this in advance and allow them to dry in shape or use semigreen or soaked willow and make it as you go.

2 Make two oval frames 12 x 14in/ 30 x 35.5cm, joining them using one of the methods on page 39 (shaving, and either lashing or tying together). If one is slightly smaller, as often happens, put this one on the inside. Arrange them so that the butt ends are coming from alternate sides, on what is to be the bottom of the basket. This evens up the weight and tensions. Decide on the shape you would like by sliding the hoops across each other. Adjusting the point at which you make the god's eye, and the length of the ribs, will significantly alter the appearance and capacity of the basket.

3 When you have marked the crossing point on both sides, in case the hoops slip when you are working, make a god's eye on each side using the hazel bark skein (see page 42).

4 For this basket you will need three ribs on each side and two on the bottom. They are all 19–20in/48–50cm long, but each basket is different and they should be carefully cut to fit at the back of the god's eye where there is a natural space for them to sit. Alternate the positions of the butt and tip ends as far as possible.

5 Measure and mark the place on the top frames (the central point of the basket) where the handle will go, and also one-third of the way from each end, where there will be a band of white weaving.

6 Begin the weave using the tip end of a long, slender, brown willow rod, working over and under each rib and twice around the hoop frame. By the time you reach the butt end of the rod you should have all the ribs securely in place. Repeat on the other side and build the weaving up in tandem on both sides of the basket.

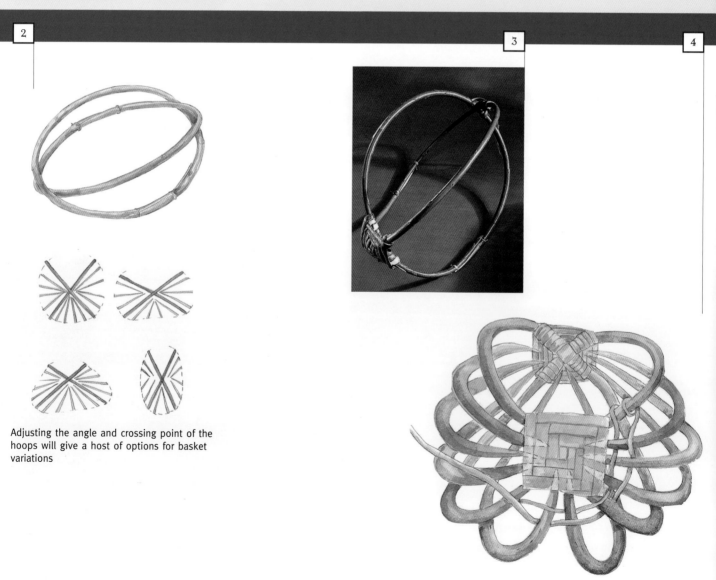

Adjusting the angle and crossing point of the hoops will give a host of options for basket variations

7 Join the randing weave in one of two ways (see page 22). (a) Either tips to tips and butts to butts using a simple join. (b) Or butts to tips, in which case you can overlap the two ends for a few strokes. The cut ends of the joins should all be on the inside of the basket. They are less likely to catch, or spring apart with any movement of the ribs this way. Avoid making a join in the gap between the top frame and the first rib, since it will not be secure.

8 Continue to weave with mixed colors of brown willow. Wrap twice around the hoop edge each time. You should be aiming at having an even parallel space across the body of the basket as soon as possible and the double wraps will partly achieve this. You may also have to pack the weave across some ribs and not others (see page 23) and you have to do this by eye until you have a straight space.

9 When you reach the first marks on the hoop, change to white willow for the next six rows of weaving.

10 Continue to weave with brown willow until you are left with a narrow gap of ½ in/1.5cm in the middle.

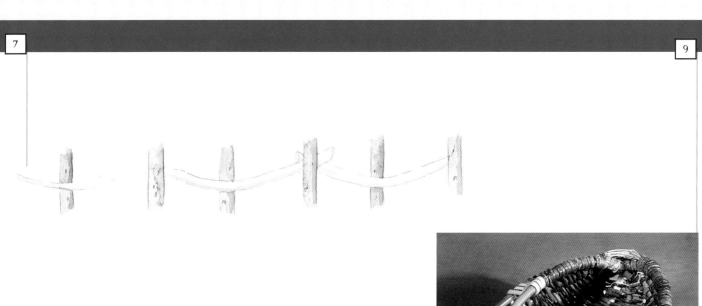

11 **Making the handle:** Use the 6ft/1.8m white rods for the handle. To make the bow, on the right-hand side, push the butt end of the stoutest rod, A, into the basket between the ribs, from outside to inside, between the frame and the first rib down. Then bring this end out over the second rib and back inside to sit firmly resting on the third rib.

12 Bend the rest of the rod over to the opposite side in a gentle curve following the profile of the melon shape of the basket. Feed it through the basket from outside to inside between the frame and the first rib. Crank the rod (see page 40), but not the part forming the bow. Bring the cranked end up to the left of the bow and wrap to your right three or four times (depending on how long the bow is) around the bow to the opposite side. Take the tip end through from the outside to the inside to the left of the bow under the frame.

13 Keeping the twist, bring the end up to the left of the bow and wrap back again to the left, following the first set.

14 Start the second rod on this (left) side, by pushing the butt end into the basket as you did for the first. Crank it and use it to wrap the handle to the right, following the groove. Follow the natural twist and bring it back to the start and then finally back again to the right. The tip ends weave away.

15 You should have the handle completely covered now. If there are any gaps, because your handle rods were not long enough, you could add another rod in the same way as the second one.

16 Work another brown weaver or two into the remaining gap in the weave The weave should meet up without an obvious join. Trim all ends neatly on the inside against a rib.

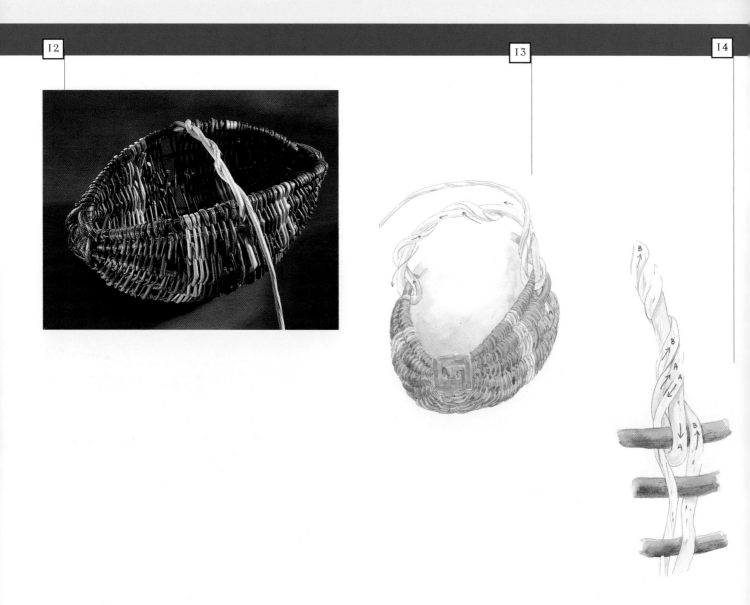

Stick Basket

It is fairly simple and fun to make this shallow basket. Materials gathered on a winter walk will make an instant and appealing container. If the basket is made from fresh materials, it will shrink after a while, and extra sticks will have to be woven in to fill the gaps. As only short sticks are needed for the central weaving, twigs of varied kinds and colors can be collected. Without the handle it makes a tray. Alternatively, two side handles can be twisted on.

You Will Need

- Four long pliable rods, at least 5ft/1.5m long to make the hoop
- Six straight rods 18in/45cm long to make the ribs
- A selection of colored "twigs" (in this basket red and green dogwood, purple-green-and-orange-barked willow were used)

- Two long pliable rods for the handle
- A knife
- A pair of shears/secateurs
- A bodkin

1 **Making the base:** The hoop can be made in whatever size suits the material you have. This basket is made on a 12in/30cm diameter hoop. Taking the first of the long rods, work on it with your thumbs until you can bend it gently into a complete circle and "tie a knot" in it. Do this by holding the butt end in your left hand and bringing the tip end through with your right hand. Now wind the tip end of the rod round and through several times, making satisfying curves without kinks.

2 Take the second rod and, placing the butt end opposite the first butt, continue to build up the hoop.

3 Now work in rods three and four, spacing the butt ends evenly round the circle.

4 Cut six ribs 4in/10cm longer than the diameter of the hoop, and lay them in two sets of three across the center. Make sure that you alternate the thick and thin ends.

5 Cut some twigs or sticks longer than the diameter of the hoop and starting in the center, place the butt end under the hoop on the right, weave it over the first set of ribs, under the second set, and let the tip end lie on top of the hoop. Immediately lay in another stick from the left, butt under the hoop and then weave to the right, exactly mirroring the first stick.

6 Continue to add sticks to either side of the central ones, alternating the thick ends, which should always be underneath the hoop. Push down on the weaving to make a dished shape. Your first efforts may turn out rather flat. The hoop tends to be pushed oval, so keep pulling it back into a circular shape. The space at the ends can be filled by thin pliable weavers, which work backward and forward wrapping over the frame.

7 Trim the ends at an angle allowing them to rest well onto the hoop.

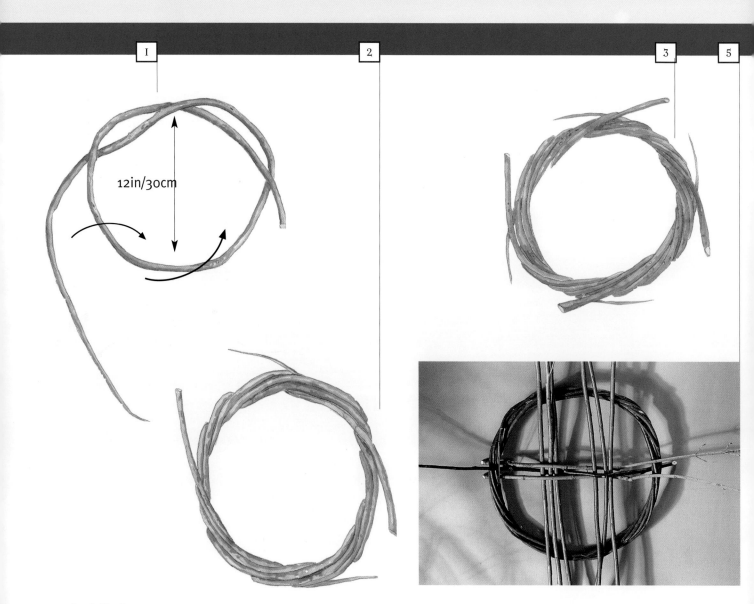

12in/30cm

8 **Making the handle:** Trim a long rod at an angle and using a bodkin push the butt end in between the wraps of the hoop next to the upper ribs on the right. Kink it up, loop it gently over to the other side and under the hoop, out in the center, and then wrap it back over itself several times back to the beginning.

9 Take the second rod and push the butt end in on the left against the lower ribs on the upper side. Kink it up and wrap it over the handle following the groove. Take it under the hoop on the other side, up the center, and wrap back to the start. Thread each tip away following the weaving of the twigs.

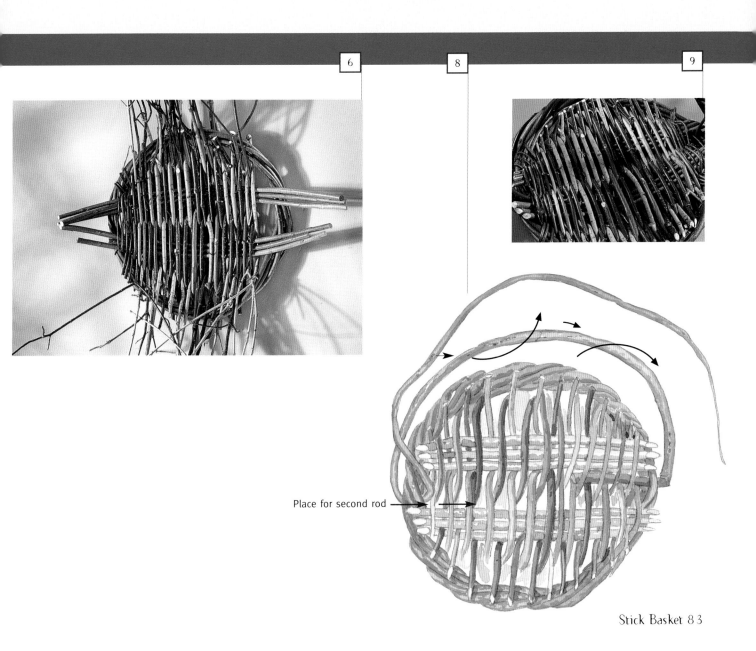

Place for second rod →

Gallery

BELOW and RIGHT: Round and oval sciathoga. Traditional Irish potato baskets woven in frame and rib technique. The colors are all natural willow. *Alison Fitzgerald.*

RIGHT: Coiled pots. Marram grass. *Molly Rathbone.*

ELOW LEFT: Resilience V – David's willow, looped. *Hisako Sekijima.*
RIGHT: A traditional Spanish basket made from Esparto grass. A wide continuous plait is sown together in a spiral.

Chair Seating

Caned Chair

This chair has a detachable seat. There are six stages of weaving in this pattern: two settings in each hole from front to back; two weavings in each hole from side to side; two crossings, running diagonally from opposite sides; it is completed with a beading, a strip of cane couched round the edge over the holes.

You Will Need

- No. 2 size chair cane for settings, weavings, and couching
- No. 3 size chair cane for crossings (about ½lb/250g of each will do several chairs, or buy a kit for one chair only)
- 39in/1m length No. 6 size chair cane for beading
- 39in/1m length No. 15 round cane for the pegs
- A knife for sharpening pegs
- Shears/secateurs for cane and pegs
- A clearing tool for clearing out old cane and tapping in new pegs (a 3in/7.5cm nail with the tip sawn off is excellent)
- A hammer for tapping in pegs
- A threading tool—a long flexible needle for working the weaving stages
- A shell bodkin—a curved and channeled tool for working the crossing stages
- Golf tees—about 24 for holding the cane in place while working (get the kind with a tapering shaft; you could use pieces of pegging cane)
- Nail clippers—with curved tips are excellent for trimming ends of cane

Project by OLIVIA ELTON BARRATT

1 **Preparation:** A chair suitable for caning has polished seat rails, with holes drilled through quite close together on each rail. Cut away any old cane and tap out the old pegs from underneath to clear the holes. Do any repairs or repolishing to the chair frame.

Chair cane can be worked dry, slightly damp, or wiped over with beeswax, whichever works best for you. Cane should not be soaked, just dampened if you wish. Sitting on an ordinary chair to work may be quite uncomfortable. Put the chair on a low platform or sit on a low stool.

2 **The first setting:** Thread a piece of No. 2 cane down through the center hole on the back rail, leaving a 6in/15cm tail below. Peg with a golf tee.

3 Bring the long end forward on top to the front rail, shiny side up; thread it down through the center hole, pull it fairly tight, and peg it.

If there are two center holes front and back, start with the left-hand ones. If there is a central hole on one rail and two on the other, then go for the straightest line.

4 Thread the cane, shiny side outward, up through the next hole on the right. Pull it tight and move the previous peg along.

5 Take the cane across and down through the next hole on the back rail. Then peg.

6 Continue until you reach the hole next to the back corner hole. Join new cane in where needed, in the hole next to the old piece. Leave 6in/15cm tails. Always keep shiny side outermost.

7 When the right side is full, start a new piece of cane next to the first peg, and work the left side. There are more holes on the longer front rail than on the back, so make "short strokes" from the remaining front holes to those on the side rails, which give the best parallel lines with the other settings. Short strokes should have tail ends in the side rails.

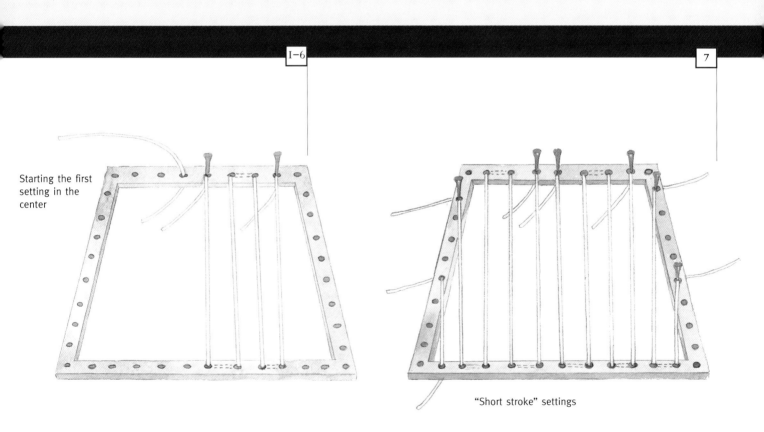

1–6

7

Starting the first setting in the center

"Short stroke" settings

HINT
Corner holes should be left empty for the crossings, but sometimes the shape of the chair forces you to use the back ones to get a good parallel line. It counts as a short stroke when working the crossings.

8 **The first weaving:** This is just laid over the first setting, not actually woven. Start at the front holes in the side rails, and use all the holes except for the corners. If there is an extra hole on one side, leave out a hole to get parallel lines. This will probably be near the back.

9 **The second setting:** Work a second setting in the same holes as the first, laid on top of the first weaving. Lay it to the right of the first in the holes, the loops underneath covering the spaces left by the first setting. No need to start in the center this time.

10 **The second weaving:** This is interwoven, using the same holes as the first weaving. Each row lies in front of its partner, under the left-hand first setting, and over the right-hand second setting. Use the cane in the direction in which it pulls without snagging. The loops underneath the frame must go in the spaces left after the first weaving. Use the threading tool, the shell bodkin, or just your fingers.

11 **To use the threading tool:** Thread it through the settings, in front of the first weaving. It goes over the right-hand setting and under the left, right across the chair.

12 Thread the tip of the cane through the eye, pinch it flat, and draw the tool back through the weave.

13 Unthread the cane and pull it through, pegging the short end in the first hole. Thread the long end down through the first hole, up through the next, pull it tight, and peg it.

14 Repeat for all holes, using the threader for each side in turn. At the holes with short strokes in them, go straight down into the hole without interweaving.

15 Keep the rows of weaving straight, and level with their own holes, pushing them down toward you. On the last two or three rows the work may be too tight to use the threader. Use your fingers for these, or the shell bodkin.

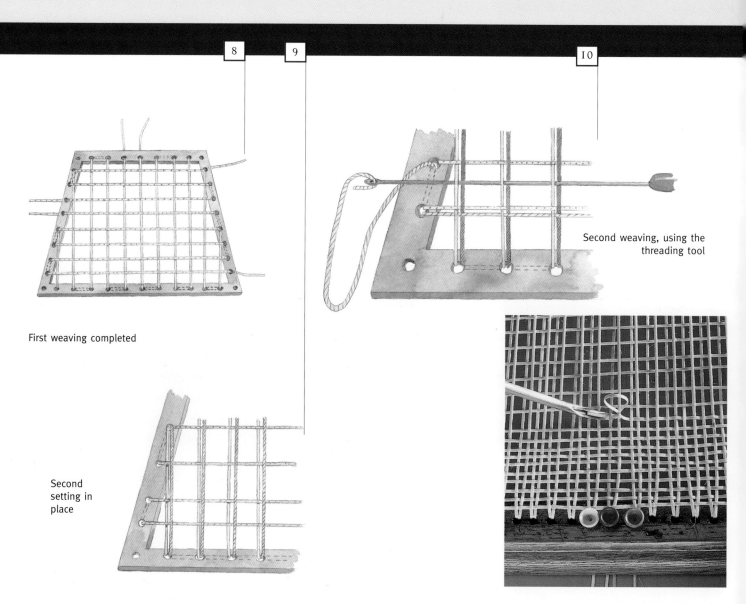

First weaving completed

Second setting in place

Second weaving, using the threading tool

The Crossings

Use No. 3 cane, and the shell bodkin, or just your fingers. Crossings run from bottom left to top right, and from bottom right to top left, interweaving with the pairs of settings and weavings. There are more holes along the front than along the sides, so crossings from side rails to the front will use some side holes twice—these are called "doubles." There are more holes in the sides than along the back, so crossings from the back rail to the side will have to leave out some side holes—these are called "misses." Corner holes are "doubled" from one way, and "missed" from the other. These doubles and misses maintain the diagonal lines.

1 **First crossing—Bottom Left to Top Right:** Weave over the settings and under the weavings. Start across the front right-hand corner, from the front rail into the side hole with no interweaving.

2 Next row goes under the first row of weaving, over the first settings, and into the next hole on the front, sliding easily across their intersection.

3 Continue like this, always going over and under the ends of the settings and weavings where they lie on the rail.

4 As there are more holes along the front than the side, make doubles (go twice) into holes immediately below the top of short strokes, and in corner holes.

5 As there are more holes in the side than the back when working from back rail to side, miss out the hole immediately below the top of a short stroke. If the work seems too tight to thread under the weavings here, make more room by pushing the short stroke inward slightly. Weave past it, and straighten it again.

6 **Second crossing—Bottom Right to Top Left:** This goes *under* the settings and *over* the weavings, interweaving with the other crossing tips to make Xs on the frame between holes. Miss out the holes with doubles in them, and double in the empty holes and the other corners. Doubles are always separated by a crossing from the other direction.

1–4

Top

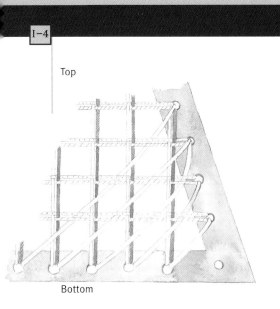

Bottom

The first crossing, showing a "double" in the hole below the short stroke

5–6

Top

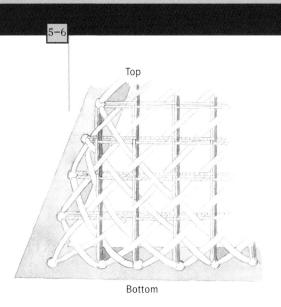

Bottom

The positions of doubles and misses, and Xs on the frame

Completed corners showing doubles and misses

Chairs made earlier than 1850–60 did not have a beaded finish, just pegs driven into every hole. After the 1850s most chairs were finished with a beading of No. 6 cane, couched (sewn down) over the holes with No. 2.

1 **The beaded finish:** Alternate holes are pegged with No. 15 round cane, with the rest left open for sewing, including the corner holes and the ones each side of them. Short ends from all open holes are brought up through neighboring holes to be secured by pegs. Cover any blank spaces underneath. You can use corner holes, but don't peg them yet.

2 **To peg the holes:** If there are an even number of holes, have two unpegged ones side by side, at one end of a rail or in the center. Tuck a piece of pegging cane into the hole (sharpened if necessary) and cut it off about ¼ in /0.5cm above the hole. Tap it down with the hammer and nail, holding projecting ends tight on top to avoid baggy loops underneath. Very slightly countersink the peg with the nail tip. It should not be long enough to stick out underneath. Peg all required holes like this (except corner holes).

3 Clip off very closely all ends of cane except for the corner holes.

4 To couch (sew) on the beading, tuck the end of a piece of No. 6 cane down into a back corner hole.

5 Thread the long end of No. 2 up through the next hole, over the No. 6, and back through the same hole. Pull it tight, under the frame and over the NO. 6, shiny side outward.

6 Repeat Step 4 to the next corner.

7 Bring the No. 2 cane up through the corner hole and thread the No. 6 down. Thread the tip of a new piece of No. 2 up. Push the end of a new piece of No. 6 down, facing along the next side. Bend it backward while you drive in a cane peg to hold all the ends tight. Countersink the peg slightly and pick off the short ends.

8 Lay the new piece of No. 6 down over the holes on the new rail, and couch along the rail as before.

9 Treat each corner in this way till you reach the last. Thread the No. 2 up and No. 6 down, and put in the final cane peg, which will show. Pick off all ends above and below.

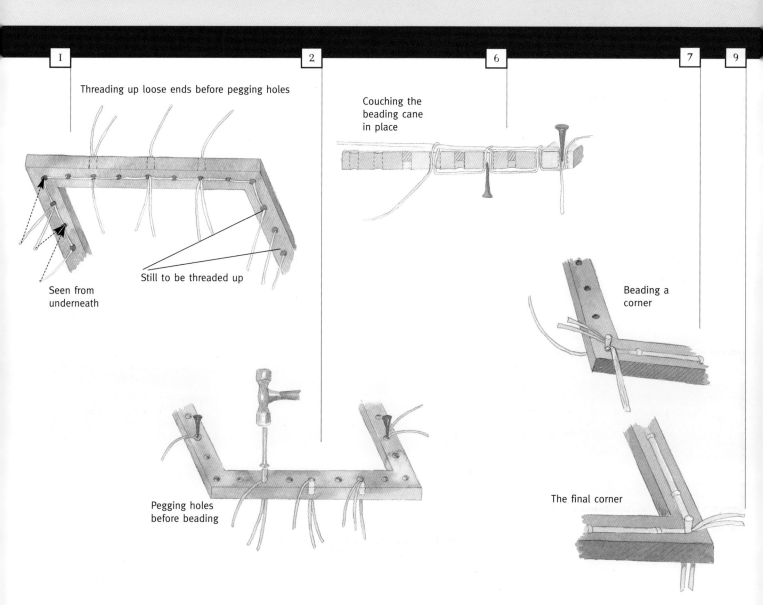

1 Threading up loose ends before pegging holes

Still to be threaded up

Seen from underneath

Pegging holes before beading

2 Couching the beading cane in place

7 9 Beading a corner

The final corner

Variations of Shape

1 Square or rectangular seats
There is no need to start the first setting in the center of the rail, since the shape is regular. The only doubles will be in the corners.

2 Curved frames
The settings are put in first to define the curve, and the tension of the weavings adjusted to maintain it. If they are too tight, they would pull the work flat across the curve. it helps to work weavings and crossings with short lengths only.

3 Rounded frames
Bow-fronted, oval, or circular, these seats have short strokes in both settings and weavings. These can be "short" at both ends, so each end causes doubles and misses, to maintain the diagonal lines.

There will be no single corner hole on a curve. A number of holes will have doubles in them.

4 Patterns
The standard pattern can be varied by using only one setting and one weaving, to give a Four-way.

Victoria patterns are quick to do, and attractive, but not as strong as the Six-way.
Their main features are:
- no doubles in the corners, but double for short strokes.
- the crossings intersect directly over the intersections of settings and weavings, giving it the nickname of Stars and Bars.

The settings, weavings, and first crossing are worked one on top of the other, and only the second crossing is interwoven. Single Victoria has only one setting and double has two. They can have a pegged or beaded edge. Beading can look more finished.

The completed final corner

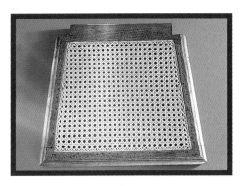

The completed trapezoid seat

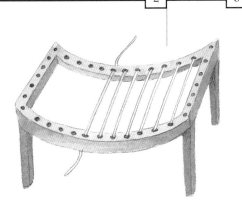

Curved frame, working both settings first to define the curve

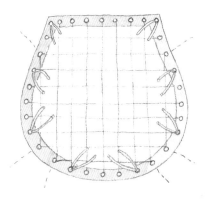

Bow-fronted frame, showing how the short strokes cause "doubles"

a) Four-way Standard

b) Single Victoria

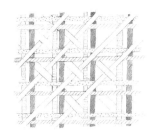

c) Double Victoria

Caned Chair 91

Willow Stool

A surprisingly strong seat in a natural material. The method used here for seating a stool can be used to restore any seat that has suitable corners to hold the weave in place. It looks best on plain, country-style furniture. You may have to scale up the willow sizes if the seat is large.

You Will Need

- Hazel or bark skein about 14ft/4.26m, or you can use thin willow rods
- 5ft/1.5m willow rods of mixed colors sorted into three weights:
  About ten stout 5ft/1.5m willow rods to be spaced in pairs at 1½–2in/3.5–5cm apart on the rails
  About twelve slightly thinner 5ft/1.5m rods for the waling

- About forty slender 5ft/1.5m willow rods for the weaving (if you want a rustic look, use gathered materials such as dogwood, elm, alder (see page 17)
- A stool (approximately 14 sq in/35 sq cm) with corners slightly proud of the rails
- Shears/secateurs
- A bodkin

1 **Wrapping the front rail:** First wrap the front rail of the seat with the hazel bark (or with thin willow rods if you are not using hazel see page 41), leaving the starting and finishing ends lying on the inside of the side rails, where they will be held in by the waling rows.

2 **Making the warp:** On the butt ends of the stout rods cut scalloms (see page 36) with 8–10in/20–25.5cm long tails on the butt ends. There must be enough tail to wrap around the rail and be held under the next two scalloms. You will need to measure your rail and work out how many rods you will need to fill the space.

3 Wrap the scalloms onto the rail in pairs as shown. This will give you a rather flatter weave than if you were to use single rods. First wrap the right-hand scallom on and then the left one, with its tail lapping over both rods.

4 To finish off the scalloms on the left edge work back the opposite way.

5 **Weaving the center:** Using the medium-thickness rods, weave a band of waling across the seat from left to right (see Stopped wale on page 28).

6 Starting at the center, use the finest of the 5ft/1.5m rods to begin the randing weave (see page 22). Work to the right. At the right-hand rail, wrap twice around before weaving back to the left. Do this on every row on both sides so that the weaving keeps level. To join on a new rod use either a tip-to-butt join OR a tip-to-tip and butt-to-butt join. Keep the ends on the back.

7 About three-quarters of the way across the seat you have to consider the finishing on the other side. The tip ends of the "warp" rods have to be wrapped around the back rail leaving enough room to work a row of waling in the gap.

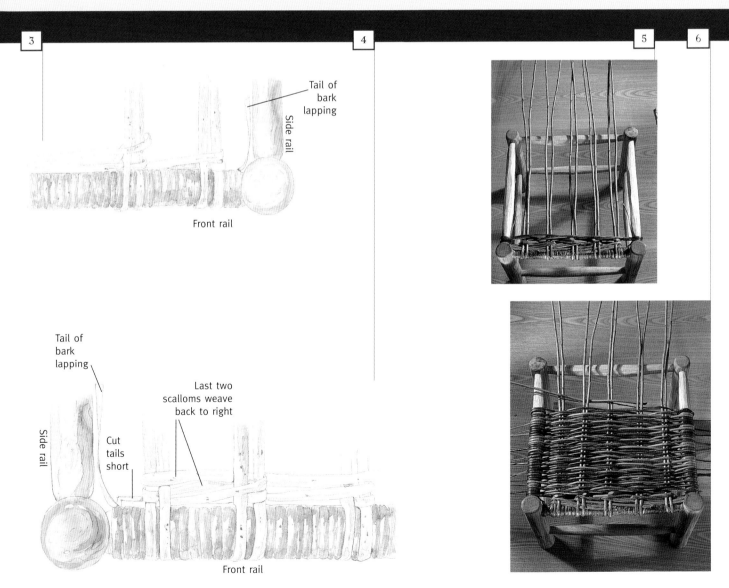

3

Tail of bark lapping

Side rail

Front rail

4

Tail of bark lapping

Last two scalloms weave back to right

Side rail

Cut tails short

Front rail

5

6

8 **Wrapping the back rail:** Begin the wrap with a slender rod (A). Place the butt end against the side rail and wrap from underneath around the rail until you meet the two stakes B and C. Lay the tail of A along the back of the rail where it will be caught in by B and C. Wrap first C under the rail and over B and C as shown, to lie along the rail. Now wrap around the rail with B and use it to wrap along the rail until it thins out. Lay the tail end along the back of the rail.

9 Now pick up C again and use it to continue the wrap along the rail. It catches in the tail of B. When you reach the next set of stakes lay C along the back of the rail and repeat the process with the new rods.

10 When you reach the right-hand edge of the stool, lay the final wrapping rod against the right-hand side rail to be caught in by the waling.

11 **Second set of waling:** Work a second row of waling to match the first above the wrapped rail using the medium-thick rods.

12 **Finishing off:** Fill in the gap which remains with randing weave using the thinnest rods. You may have to crank the last rods (see page 40) to make them supple in order to thread them into the small gap at the end. Turn the stool over to trim all the ends neatly against a stake. Leave the seat to dry thoroughly before using the stool or you may distort the weave.

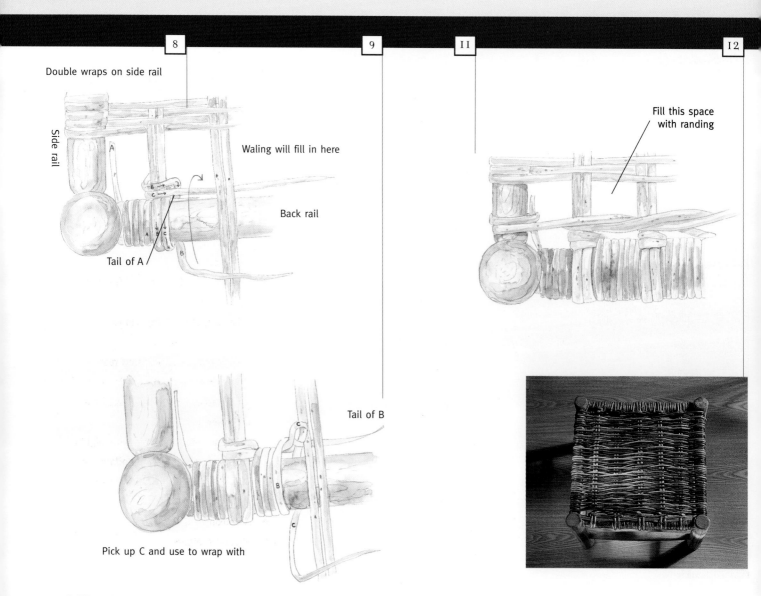

8

9

11

12

Double wraps on side rail

Side rail

Waling will fill in here

Back rail

Tail of A

Fill this space with randing

Tail of B

Pick up C and use to wrap with

Willow and Rush Stool

My thanks go to Brigitte Stone, a professional chair seater, for the design of this unusual weave. It has a very satisfying combination of materials and textures, and, although the plain weave is very simple, the spacing of the thinner willow rods against the wider rush plait gives a diagonal twill effect. The soft rush makes for a comfortable seat while the willow gives it added strength.

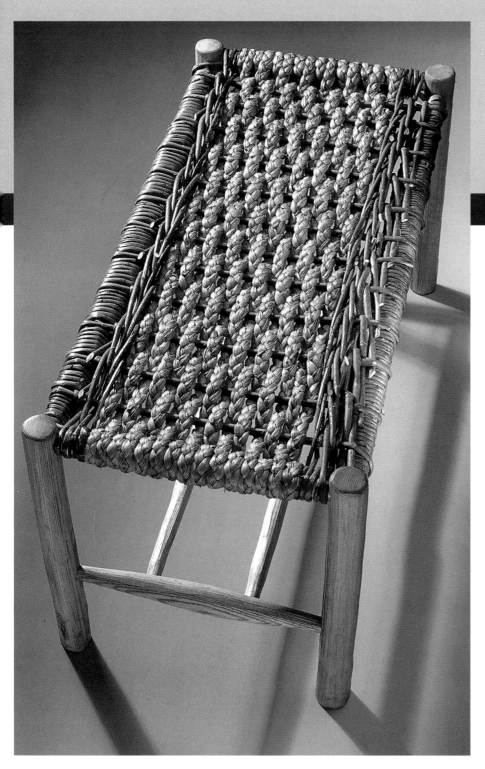

You Will Need

- Twelve stout 6ft/1.8m brown willow rods to set them 1½–2in/3.5–5cm apart on the long front rail
- About twenty four finer 5ft/1.5m rods for the waling
- A handful of finer 4ft/1.2m rods for wrapping the front rail
- A large bundle of prepared rush (approximately half a bolt for a stool) All materials should be soaked and mellowed
- A suitable stool or chair, with slightly raised corners to accommodate the weave and prevent it slipping off
- A sharp knife
- A bodkin
- Shears/secateurs

I **Wrapping the rails and scalloming on the willow rods:** Wrap the long rail at the front of the stool, with slender 4ft/1.2m willows (see page 41). Lay the starting and finishing ends against the side rails to be caught in by the subsequent rows of waling.

2 Cut long scalloms (see page 36) on the butt ends of the stout rods and attach them to the front rail by wrapping them on, setting them approximately 2in/5cm apart. The ones closest to the right and left sides should be slightly nearer to the rails for added strength (approximately 1½ in/3.5cm). The last scallom should wrap back in the opposite direction and weave over the others.

3 Waling (see page 28). Using the waling weavers, complete one row each of waling and "reverse" waling on top of the scalloms to hold them in.

4 The stakes forming the "warp" must now be wrapped at the opposite side, onto the back rail. Start to wrap the back rail with a spare willow rod. This will look neat if you crank the willow first (see page 40). Wrap on the first warp rod as if it were a scallom, catching in the end of the first wrapping rod and then using it as the next wrap. Repeat with all the other stakes. Crank all the ends of the stakes to make them more supple.

5 Weave rows of waling and "reverse" waling above this to match the other side. This is slightly more difficult because of the fixed stakes. Trim all the ends neatly.

6 **The rush plait (see plaiting on page 44):** Take three rushes and lay them out with two butts and a tip at one end and the opposite at the other. Begin the plait at a point where all the rushes are fairly similar in size, leaving a long starting tail. Make a section of three-strand plait long enough to wrap twice around the left-hand side rail twice with an inch/2.5cm to spare at the front end.

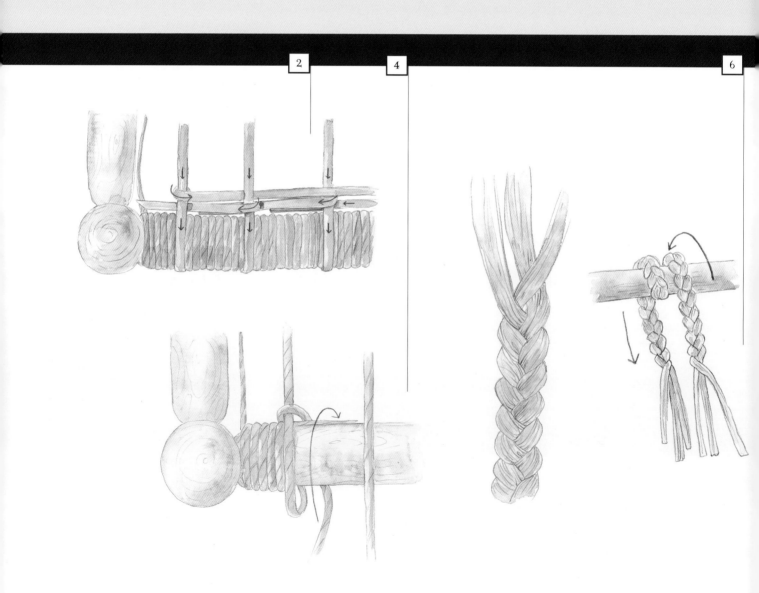

7 Bring the two ends of the plait together and lay the right over the left joining them in a single plait. The "loop" of the plait must be at the left front, on the side nearest the waling. Then continue to plait.

8 You will need to add new rushes regularly to keep the width of the plait even. Make enough at a time to stretch over to the opposite side plus 12in/30cm. Then pull on it, and give it a good stretch, to straighten it, and prevent it from becoming slack in the seat. Trim any loose ends where you have joined on.

9 Weave a plain, over-one, under-one weave, over to the right-hand side. Weave in and out loosely all the way from one side to the other, then adjust and tighten the weave. Continue to add rushes and plait another length long enough to stretch back to the left-hand side of the stool. Wrap around the right-hand rail twice before making the opposite weave back to the left. Work an opposite weave under-one, over-one through the "warp" rods. Continue to work backward and forward across the seat, wrapping twice around the side rails until you cannot pack any more rows in. Leave a few inches spare for the finish.

10 Finishing off: Turn the stool upside down. Use the bodkin to make a space and thread the end of the braid away under two or three of the wraps against the rail so that it is held very firmly in place and will not slip out. Allow the willow and rush to dry completely in a warm, well-ventilated room before you use it, or the seat may be pulled out of shape.

HINT
After allowing the plait to dry out, you may find there is room for an extra row.

Elm Bark Seat

If you are able to get access to the right kind of trees, then bark seating is a relatively cheap and attractive way to seat chairs. The technique below can also be adapted to make baskets and, once you have gained a feel for working with bark, there is no end to the other applications for which it can be used. If you are unable to harvest the bark itself, then you should be able to buy it. You should be using the inner bark of hickory, wych elm, or possibly lime. The strips for this chair have a total surface area of about five times the area of the seat. The weave will run in both directions over the top of the seat and in both directions over the bottom, thus covering the seat four times. You then need to allow some extra for corners, knots, and waste. The chair used can be an old one that needs restoring or you may wish to make a new one.

Project by MIKE & TAMSIN ABBOTT

You Will Need

- 10 sq.ft/9 sq.m of bark to cover approximately 2 sq.ft/1.8 sq.m of seat. If the strips are cut 1in/2.5cm wide, this will require 120ft/36.5m
- One chair on which to apply the seating
- A sharp knife
- A blunt flexible knife, such as a table knife
- A "prodder"—a square-ended length of wood, the width of a bark strip
- Boiled linseed oil and brush to apply
- If the bark has been dried, you will need a bowl of warm water and some rags

1 If the bark has been dried, you should soak it in warm water for one or two hours. It is best to remove it all from the water, unwrap the coils, and wipe them dry with a rag and leave the bark for an hour or so before use. If the bark is fresh from the tree, it can be used without any preparation.

2 Select your first length of bark. Start with the longer lengths, saving the shorter lengths for the more fiddly weaving. Cut the first 4in/10cm to a width of about ½ in/1.5cm. Tie this with a simple looped knot around the end of the left-hand side of the rear seat rails. When bark dries out it will stiffen in position, and any knots will be locked into place.

Then wrap the length of bark under the seat with the outside surface of the bark facing downward. Bring it around and over the front seat rail so now the outside of the bark is uppermost. As the bark dries, it will shrink but it will also curl away from the outer side. If the bark is woven with the inner surface on top, the edges will curl upward and it will be less comfortable to sit on. Now take the bark so as to cover your first knot. Don't worry about the triangular corner of the seat until the end. Keep wrapping the bark backward and forward square to the front and rear seat rails until you have used up the first length. Cut this so that it ends beneath the seat. As at the start, cut a 4in/10cm narrow section at the end.

3 **To join on a length:** tie two lengths together using a weaver's knot as illustrated. Take a new length and again cut a narrow section at the end. Fold the 3in/7.5cm of each strip back on itself to form two loops. Holding them at right angles, feed one loop through the other so that it projects about ½ in/1.5cm (Fig. 3a).

Take the loose end of the outer loop and wrap it up, around and back over itself, so that it points in the same direction as the other loop (Fig. 3b).

Tuck this end through the inner loop and gently pull the knot tight by pulling the thick ends of the strips in opposite directions (Fig. 3c).

4 Continue working across the seat, making sure that any knots are tied beneath the seat and that the strips are kept fairly taut. When you reach the right-hand rear corner, wrap the bark over the rear seat rail, around the leg, under the seat, and bring it out around the right-hand seat rail.

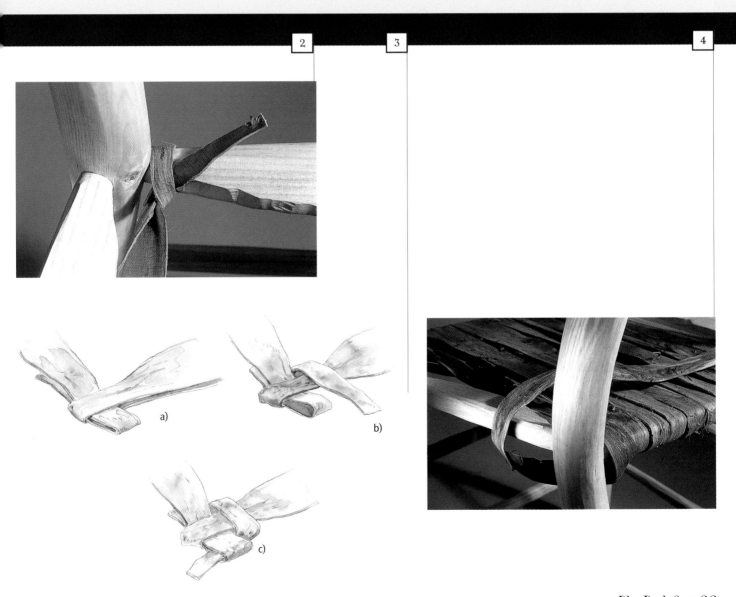

a)

b)

c)

5 The herringbone pattern for the weave requires concentration. Start at the back of the seat on the right. The first row is alternately over two then under two. It is just as easy to weave a herringbone on the underside as well, repeating the over two and under two. The second row starts by going over just one strip but then continues under two and over two, repeating the pattern of the first row, but one strip sideways. The third row starts by going straight under two, then over two, and so on. The fourth row starts under one before continuing over two, under two. The fifth row now repeats the first and so on until the front of the seat is reached. Again, the knots should be tied on the underside, and, with practice, you should be able to hide them completely.

6 After completing the first few rows across the seat, you may find that the strips start to lose a straight line, so you should straighten them by pushing them toward the back. This is where the prodder is used to get them back into line. The last few rows are awkward to weave in and out, so you will find it helpful to use a blunt knife to slide in between the bark strips, opening up a gap for the new weaving. When both side rails have been covered, cut off the last strip after weaving halfway across the underside. When dry, it stays put.

7 At this stage, the triangular corners are still empty. To do the job properly, you should now leave the seat in a warm room for a day or two for the bark to dry out, since the strips will loosen up to a quarter of their width in the process, creating gaps between them. You then use the prodder to push the strips tight up together again. Push the front to back strips toward the left and feed in another couple of rows on the right. Feed in a couple of side to side rows as well to fill the gaps. The corners are now filled by weaving in short strips of bark from front to back. These will not be supporting much weight and therefore do not need to be tied to the original strips.

8 **Finishing off:** When the bark is dry, brush over with two coats of boiled linseed oil.

5

6

7

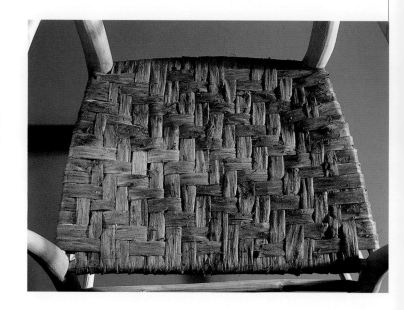

Square Rush Seat

Rushes are twisted together to form a smooth continuous coil, with more added as required to keep it even in size. It is wound around the seat rails from corner to corner, gradually filling in the open space and finishing in the middle. The size of coil varies according to the chair: thicker for heavier chairs, thinner for finer styles. It forms a top and bottom layer on the frame, and the space between is tightly stuffed with dry rushes for comfort and hard wear. If you cannot find rushes, cattails are a good substitute.

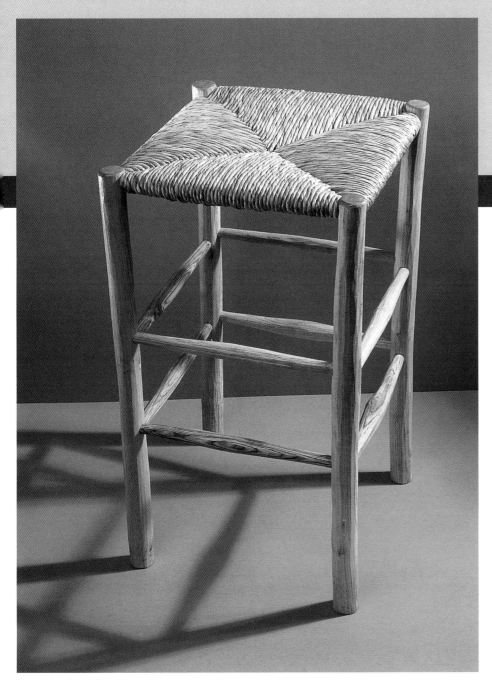

You Will Need

- A bolt of rush will seat more than one chair
- A rush threader for pulling coils through in the final stages, use a sacking needle with a large eye, or heavy gauge wire bent into a tight U with the ends bound to form a handle
- A stuffing stick for stuffing the seat with waste rushes, and packing coils together (or a piece of hardwood battening with one end sanded thin and rounded off)
- A wooden dolly for ironing down the completed coils for a well-finished look
- Scissors
- A tape measure or rule

Project by OLIVIA ELTON BARRATT

1 **Preparation:** A seat suitable for rushing has unpolished rails joined to the raised corner posts, and an open center. Cut away any old rushes, and do any repairs necessary to the chair frame, making sure the rails are smooth. Water a bundle of rush with a hose or watering can, and wrap it tightly in a thick damp cloth for at least three hours to mellow and absorb the water.

2 **Working position:** Preferably sit on a seat lower than the chair to be rushed, with the chair on the floor in front of you. Your back stays straight, and you can use your legs to grip the chair, leaving your hands free for maintaining tension on the rush coil.

3 **Starting the rush coil:** Tie a piece of string around a leg to mark corner 1. The front rail is between corners 1 and 2. With corner 1 to your right, loop a long rush around the back rail close to the corner at 4, bringing both ends together over the front rail. Using a half-hitch knot, pulled really tight, join on enough rush by the butts (the thick ends) to make the required size of coil.

4 With the rushes lying to your right, twist them all together with your right hand, away from you and corner 1, making a firm coil. Coil down the length of the rushes, your left hand following up to smooth and compress. The coil must be smooth. Make it the required size by adding or taking away rushes.

5 Coil far enough to go over the front rail, and underneath for about 1in/2.5cm. (The rushes under the seat remain untwisted, to hold the stuffing better.) Pull the coil tight, lay it over the front rail next to the corner, and bring it up in the center space. Turn the chair clockwise so the coil points to your left over the side rail. Use your left hand to twist the coil toward you and the corner, following up with your right. Pull it tight and make a good right-angle turn over the first coil. Lay it over the side rail against the corner, and bring it up in the center space. The actual coil will still be twisting the same direction—check and see.

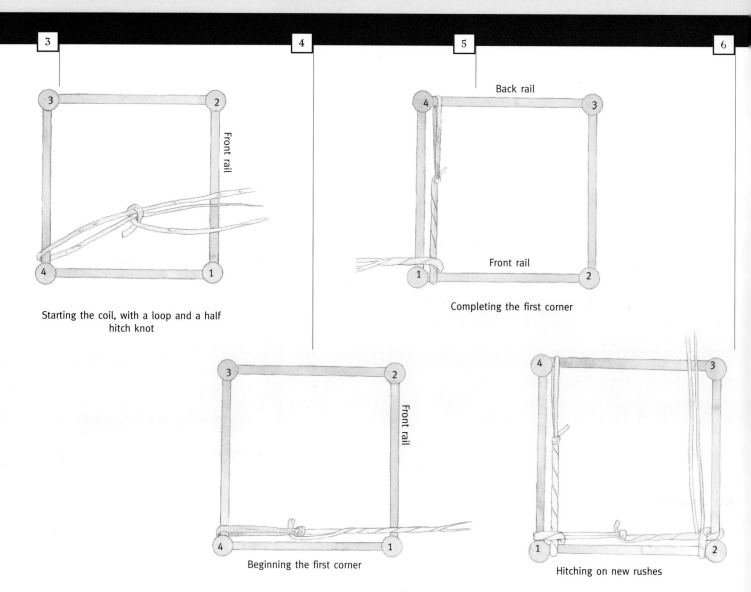

Starting the coil, with a loop and a half hitch knot

Beginning the first corner

Completing the first corner

Hitching on new rushes

6 Maintain the size of the coil by half-hitching on new rushes when needed, keeping the knot away from the corners. Start coiling near the next corner. Repeat for each corner round the seat, adding new rushes when needed. Keep the coils even in size. At the last corner, make sure the coils cover up the first loop of rush.

7 **Working the seat:** As the work progresses, you will also need corner joins to maintain thickness. Complete the first half of the corner and bring the coil up in the center. Lay in a new butt on the right of the working coil, and twist it invisibly in with the coil. Complete the corner.

8 When rushes dry, they shrink looser, so, as you work round the chair, pull each coil very tight before you lay it down, and press it hard in toward the corner. This helps to keep good tension and right angles to avoid unsightly wedge-shaped center gaps, which are difficult to correct.

9 As the gap in the center fills up, there is no room for half-hitches. Join in new rush by tucking butts into the under-seat pocket, starting to coil old and new rush together where they emerge to cross the center space.

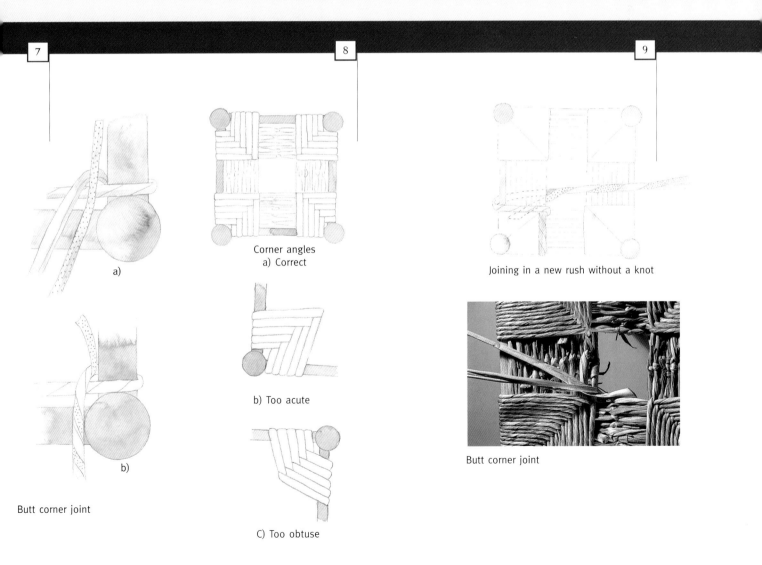

7

a)

b)

Butt corner joint

8

Corner angles
a) Correct

b) Too acute

C) Too obtuse

9

Joining in a new rush without a knot

Butt corner joint

10 The seat is complete when no more complete rounds can be worked, even by pushing the coils tightly in to the corners. Be very careful not to lose the correct sequence as the central gap closes. Finish at the end of a round, that is, over the back rail at corner 4. Take the coil over the back rail and tuck it tightly into the under-seat pocket, toward corner 3.

11 Stuffing can be done as the work progresses if you have to work in short spells, with the chair drying out between sessions. Use the stuffing stick to pack dry rushes into the pockets under the seat on each side of the corner. Stuff the central areas after completion.

12 If the chair is completed over one or two days, and is still damp:

• Turn the chair on its side, and stuff away from you into the underside pockets on the right, working first from the center to the furthest corner, and then from the nearest corner to the center. When the pockets are tightly filled, repeat with the other three sides.
• Avoid stretching damp coils by levering them up with the stick. Keep it as flat as possible against the seat.

13 Turn the seat over, and check if any coils are standing up proud. If so, use the stick to push the neighboring coils away to make more room. Now iron down firmly with the dolly from the edges to the center. It helps the coils to stay down and gives a neat finish. This works best on damp coils. Tuck away all the protruding ends underneath the seat.

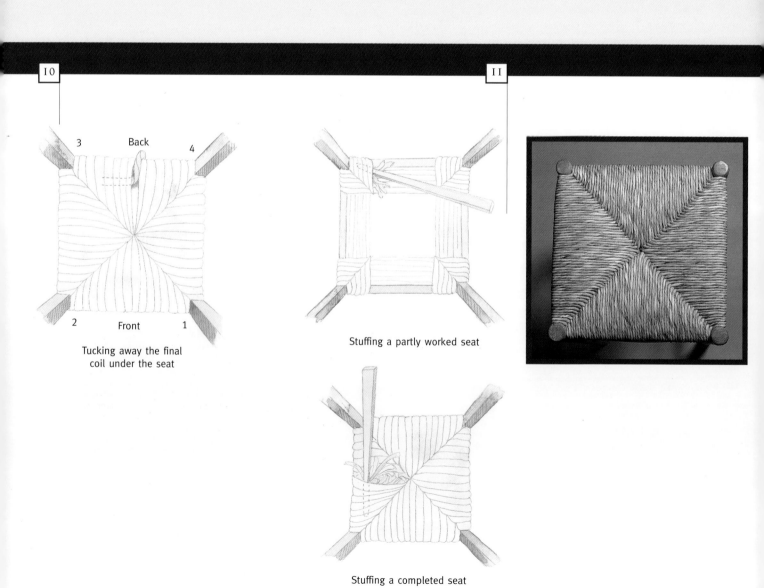

Tucking away the final
coil under the seat

Stuffing a partly worked seat

Stuffing a completed seat

Variations

1 Rectangular seats
The short side rails fill up before the long front and back rails, leaving a central gap. When the short rails are filled, finish at the end of a round, and fill in the gap with a figure-of-eight sequence from one long rail to the other, finishing at the other end, over the back rail. This is called a "bridge." Pack the bridge coils together at intervals, and fit in as many as you can. Stuff and finish as before.

2 Trapezoid seats—wider fronts than backs
These require a technique called "doubling to fill in the extra space on the front rail. "

3 Trapezoid seats: Work the two front corners, and tie off the coil temporarily to the side rail.

4 Half-hitch enough rushes for a new coil onto the first at the start, and work the two front corners again.

5 Untie the first coil and take rushes from both to make a single coil. Work the two back corners with this, trimming off any discarded rushes. These three steps give two coils on the front corners for every one on the back.

6 Double on every round until the gaps on the front and back rails are the same size, measured at the end of a round. Then work the rest of the seat without doubling. This shape may end exactly in the center, or with a bridge, depending on dimensions. It helps to have a half-hitch on the first coil of each doubling round, so that you can hitch the second coil on behind it to prevent it slipping.

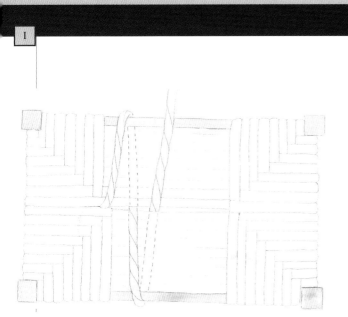

Starting the bridge on a rectangular stool

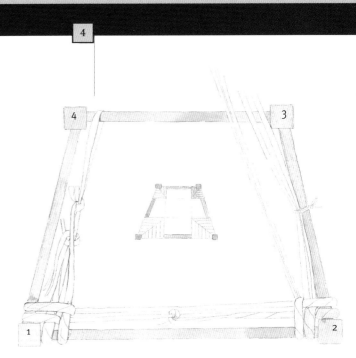

The first round of "doubling" on a trapezoid seat

Detail of seagrass rectangular seat

Gallery

LEFT: A freeform chair in Laburnum. Seats woven in coiled rush. *Gudrun Leitz.*

BELOW: Round table with a central medallion. Using the six-way chair seating pattern worked in a complex way. *Brigitte Stone.*

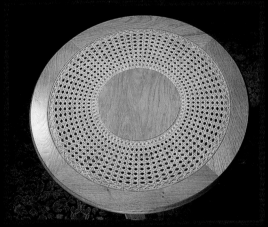

BELOW: **Samurai**—a chair to curl up in. Made from the sustainable resources of cultivated willow from Somerset, and coppiced ash from Dorset. *Guy Martin.*

ABOVE: **Soetsu**—a stool for good posture. Designed to minimalize back fatigue. *Guy Martin.*

Outdoor Structures

Spiral Plant Support

Use dip-dyed or plain-colored cane to make a support for climbing pot plants. The spiraling loops are wound around and threaded through a strong dowel. Brightly colored beads cover the two ends of the cane.

You Will Need

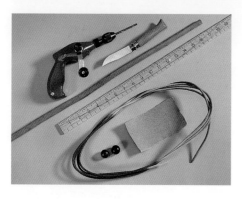

- One length of dip-dyed No. 14 center cane 130in/3.3m long. Dyed with green, turquoise, and maroon fabric dyes
- A stout stick or doweling ½in/1.5cm diameter, 25in/63.5cm long
- Two 1in/2.5cm colored beads to match the cane

- Turquoise, maroon, and green dye
- A hand drill and ³⁄₁₆in/10.5cm bit
- A ruler
- A knife
- Sandpaper

1 **How to dip-dye the cane:** Tie the cane in a loop with the middle tightly tied into a waist. Dip one end into turquoise dye made up following the supplier's instructions and leave it to take up the color while the dye boils for 20 minutes. Remove and rinse off excess dye in cold water.

2 Turn the loop around and dye the other end with maroon dye in the same way. Undo the central tie and retie the canes squashing it the other way so that you can dye the other ends. Dye both of these green, one after the other, leaving a space of undyed cane between each of the colors. If you are using the cane immediately it will be pliable from the boiling. If not, allow it to dry thoroughly in a warm place.

3 **Making the support:** Take the stick and, starting 2in/5cm from the top, mark four places at 4in/10cm intervals. Now turn it so that you are at right angles to these, and mark four places starting 4in/10cm from the top. Keep the same intervals so that these marks come halfway between the previous ones.

4 Clamp the stick securely so that you can drill holes at these spacings right through the stick. Sand down any splinters lightly.

5 Taking one end of the cane, thread it through the top hole leaving 1in/2.5cm protruding. Now wind the length of the cane in a clockwise direction in a loose loop round the stick, making almost a complete circle, and thread it through the next hole down.

6 Repeat the process, working down the stick and widening the loops as you go, and making pleasing curves. The end of the cane should reach the last hole and push through as at the top. Adjust the cane to fit.

7 Trim the top and bottom ends of the center cane into a point so that you can push the beads firmly onto them. Trim the top of the stick to a neat angle without sharp edges. Shave the bottom end to a point so that it can easily be pushed into a plant pot.

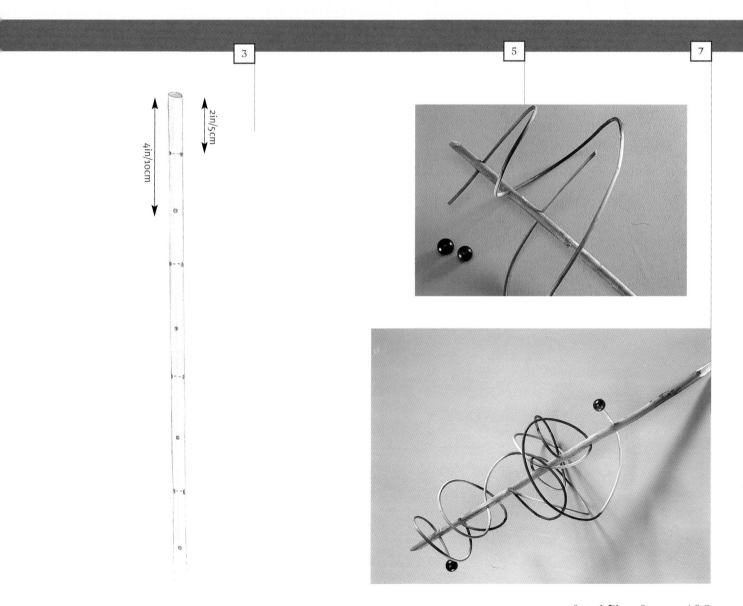

2in/5cm

4in/10cm

Conical Plant Support

A simple structure to support climbing plants in the garden. The jig is not strictly necessary to make the project. You can push uprights into the ground, and walk around it as you weave. If you are making a few supports, a jig will save a lot of bending, and you can sit comfortably still and spin the project instead.

Project by ANDY SOUTHWELL

You Will Need

FOR THE JIG

- ³⁄₈in/9mm plywood, 32 x 16in/81 x 40.5cm
- Wood plank 8 x 16 x 1in/ 20 x 40.5 x 2.5cm
- ⁵⁄₈in/15mm wide dowel,1¹⁄₂in/3.5cm long
- Four x 1in/2.5cm screws
- Wood glue
- Sandpaper
- A jigsaw
- A drill and bits
- A screwdriver
- A pair of compasses

FOR THE SUPPORT

- Ten 7–9ft/2.1–2.75m straight, thick, brown, unsoaked willow rods for the uprights
- Thirteen 5–6ft/1.5–1.8m brown willow rods for the weavers
- Shears/secateurs
- A bodkin
- Rapping wood
- A tape measure
- A rubber tie

Making the jig: The plant-support jig is a fairly straightforward woodworking project if you have the tools and materials available.

1 Draw two 16in/40.5cm circles on the plywood and cut out the circles with the jigsaw. Cut the plank in half to make two 8in/20cm squares. Sandwich one of these centrally between the two plywood circles and screw together with two screws from the top and two staggered from the bottom. Make sure they are countersunk flush to the surface of the wood to allow the jig to spin freely.

2 Drill a ⅝in/1.5cm hole ¾in/2cm deep into the center of the other square of wood and glue in the dowel.

3 Drill a hole ¾in/2cm deep into the center of the plywood circles. To ensure that the dowel spins freely, drill the hole slightly oversize, or sand down the dowel to fit loosely. You can help the bearing to spin by rubbing it with candle wax. Draw two circles at 10in/25.5cm and 12in/30cm diameter on the top of the jig. Drill through the top layer only 10 x ⅜in/1cm holes equally spaced on the smaller circle, and 12 on the larger one.

4 **Making the plant support:** Make points on the butt ends of the 10 thick rods with the hand-held pruning shears —or secateurs—and push the butts into the 10in/25.5cm circle of the jig.

5 Tie the tops together with a temporary tie. The uprights are held in place by three woven bands made using the following pairing weave, which has an extra twist because of the large space between the uprights.

6 Take two of the weavers, and, 15in/38cm up from the base, place the tips in two adjacent spaces between the uprights. Leaving 12in/30cm of the tips pushed inside and holding the weavers in your left hand, bring the left weaver in front of the upright and cross it over its partner.

7 Now take both weavers in your right hand the other side of the crossover and twist them clockwise over each other to make a double twist.

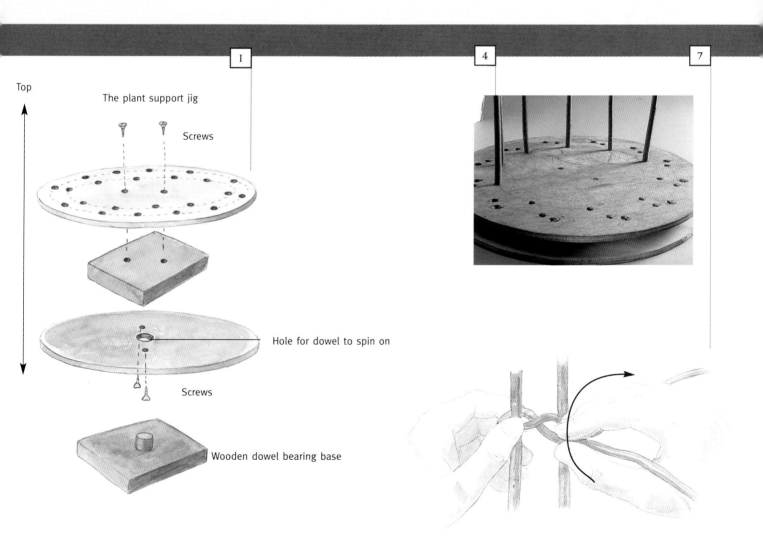

Top

The plant support jig

Screws

Screws

Hole for dowel to spin on

Wooden dowel bearing base

8 Pass the second weaver behind the next upright so that they are back in adjacent spaces. Note that one weaver always passes behind each upright and the other in front of the uprights.

9 Continue with this weave until you reach the butts. Try to keep the weaving level and the spacing between the uprights even, and make the weavers twist evenly over each other. Join the butt using a pairing join (see page 24). Notice that there is no double twist in the two spaces where you should make the join.

10 Continue weaving to within 12in/30cm of the tip of the rod. The starting and finishing tips then form two wraps around the whole band of weaving. Tuck in the tips to stop them unwrapping.

11 Weave two more bands in the same way, spacing them 8in/20cm apart. The willow rods will make three rows of weaving on the top band. Taper the support by making the spaces between the uprights progressively smaller as you go up. Finally secure the top with a willow wrap (see page 40).

Variations

You can make the plant supports larger or smaller by increasing the number of uprights and the diameter of the circle. A 3ft 6in/1m support would have eight supports around an 8in/20cm base. A 6ft/1.8m has 12 uprights round a 12in/30cm base. It is a good idea to bring the supports inside during the winter to extend their life.

8 9 10 11

Peacock

A peacock has several distinctive features, and these instructions could be used with some alteration to make other birds. The success of the project will depend on your eye for searching out the right material. It helps if you can find a model, and spend some time looking at its form and making rough sketches. Try to break down the shape into basic spheres, blocks, and triangles, and decide what the striking features are. You can make this peacock where you intend to display it, by pushing the legs into the ground, otherwise you will have to arrange a support for the legs.

You Will Need

- Large sticks for the framework of the body. I used four large branches, which should not be straight; look for suitably curved shapes that will lend themselves to the body shape. The diameter of the thick end was at least 1in/2.5cm
- Two large-branched sticks for the legs. Look for forked branches that will imitate the leg joints. This will make the bird look as if it is stepping along. The diameter of the thick end should be 1–1½ in/2.5–3.5cm
- Five or six flat-branched rods for the tail

- A large bundle of smaller pliable weavers to make the hoops, and for weaving the body. They should be at least 5–6ft/1.5–1.8m long, approximately 60
- Thin galvanized wire
- Shears/secateurs
- A drill and bits
- Pliers
- A saw
- A knife

1 **Making the framework:** First make a strong and stable framework for your bird. Set the legs at different angles to each other and at least 8in/20cm apart both back to front and side to side, in order to balance the body. The leg branches should continue up into the body, one toward the head and the other toward the tail end.

2 More strong branches make the body structure. Use four to make a strong oblong box-like framework. This should not be too large, the hoops forming the outline of the body shape go over it, and the framework should fit inside the body shape. Onto this, wire the legs in several places so that the whole structure is strong and stable enough to take the weight of the finished weaving. To attach the wire, cut a length 12in/30cm long, wind it several times around the branches, then, using pliers, twist the two ends together until all the slack is taken up. Fold the twisted end flat against the branch, so that you will not cut yourself on it. To make the leg join more secure, you can drill a small hole right through the branches, and wire through this. The cut ends of wire are very sharp, so take care not to scratch or cut yourself on them when weaving.

3 **Making the body structure with hoops:** Make five hoops in several sizes. Each one is made by twisting two willow rods into a circle (see Stick Basket project page 82, stages 1 and 2). The three body hoops are 10-12in/25-30cm, the one at the tail end is 7in/17-18cm, and the smaller one at the neck end is 15½in/12.5cm.

4 Keep working on the structure until you are satisfied that it has the skeleton you have in mind. Fill the hollow of the body with some loose twiggy branches to provide something for your weavers to work into.

5 Wire on a few "outline" weavers to give you a guide to the shape. At this stage you can make a rough neck, tail, and head so that the whole of the bird is starting to emerge. The neck should be kept slender.

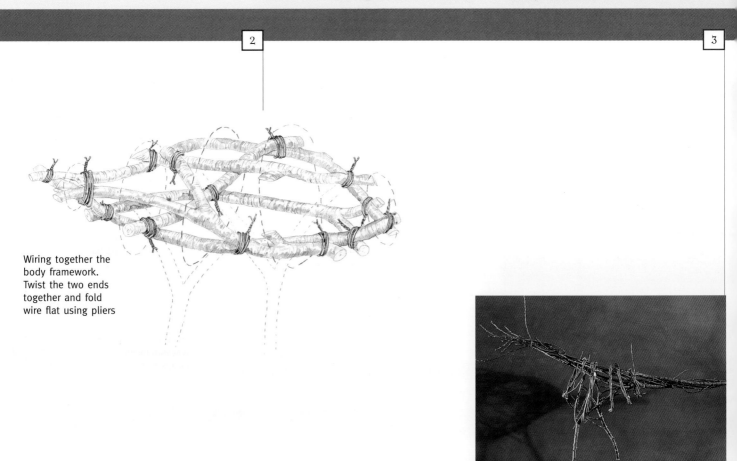

2

3

Wiring together the body framework. Twist the two ends together and fold wire flat using pliers

Wire the hoops firmly onto the bird in several places

6 To make the head, decide where to bend down two of the weavers coming up from the neck. Make them into a V-shape for the beak. Don't make this too big or it will look clumsy. Do not finish it at this stage—you just need to decide on the general shape.

7 **Forming the legs:** Make the thighs of the bird by wrapping (see page 40) the butt ends of several rods onto the upper part of the legs. These rods give strength to the legs and you should attach them firmly to the hoops or structure of the framework. Divide the branches you have chosen and weave between them in a figure-of-eight to make a convincing thigh.

8 **Weaving the body:** Begin to weave both sides of the body by pulling the tip ends of weavers over and under the hoops, using them as a "warp." Thread the tip ends in opposite directions and then pull them hard to bring the butt ends along. Aim to use the tips for the tail and neck so that they do not become too thick too quickly. Using the butt ends for the bulk of the body will fill up the gaps.

9 Build up the weaving on the sides, underneath, and on top in the same way. On the front, take the butt ends round across the front of the body in a curve and push them to the inside to make a chest. At the back, spread them into the beginnings of a tail. On top, take the weavers right around to the other side to make shoulders. Try to have a flow that suggests the shape of the bird. Leave a space on the top at the back for the tail.

10 When you have filled up all the space on the hoops, work on the neck and the tail.

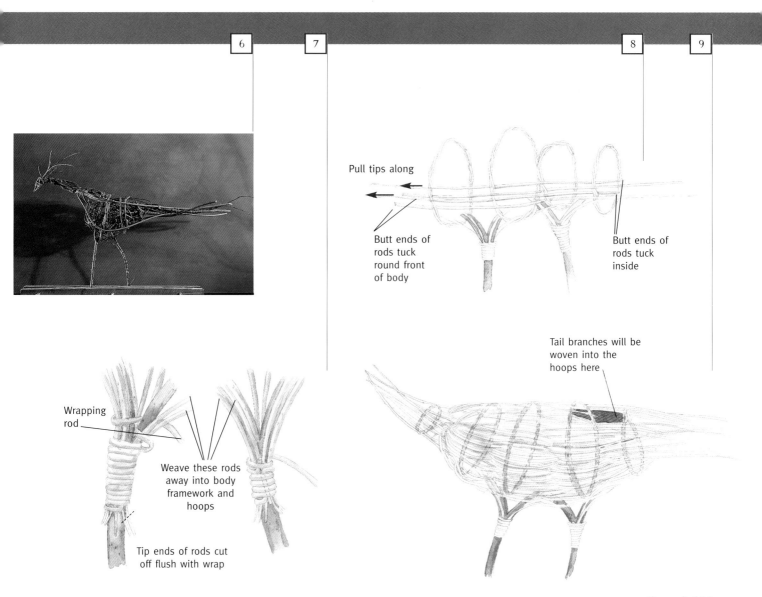

Pull tips along

Butt ends of rods tuck round front of body

Butt ends of rods tuck inside

Tail branches will be woven into the hoops here

Wrapping rod

Weave these rods away into body framework and hoops

Tip ends of rods cut off flush with wrap

11 **The tail:** Look for some suitable branched material for a tail. Some trees grow in a fanlike pattern with lateral branches which spread flat in two directions only. I used five or six pieces of elm which have been gently bent down into a curve following the sweep of the tail. Push these between the hoops, into the space at the back of the bird, so that they form the back and tail.

12 Using pairing, (see page 24), weave several rows across the tail, so that the tip ends of the body weavers are held in with the new branches.

13 **The head:** Refine the beak and weave a slender rod backward and forward to fill the space. Make the comb by bending backward some of the tips coming up from the neck. Wrap around them to make them stay in place.

14 Make an eye on each side of the head. Push a thin willow rod into the head and crank it. Make a loop. Wind the willow tightly round and round the loop and then thread the tip end through to stop it unraveling. Thread the tip away. Use your imagination.

15 Tidy up any loose ends, making a clean outline of your bird.

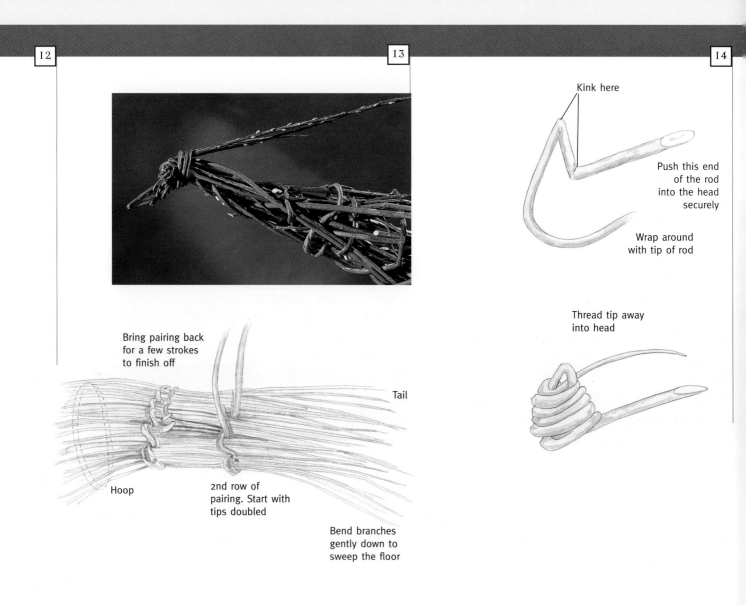

12

13

14

Bring pairing back for a few strokes to finish off

Hoop

2nd row of pairing. Start with tips doubled

Tail

Bend branches gently down to sweep the floor

Kink here

Push this end of the rod into the head securely

Wrap around with tip of rod

Thread tip away into head

Arbor

You can use these instructions to construct various domed shapes. This one is large enough for several people to stand inside, and has a doorway and a porch. The size you make it will depend on space and the availability of materials. To make something as large as the one shown here you will need a lot of chunky material and the energy to bend it. It helps to have someone hold the rods in place as you weave— and to offer encouragement.It is staked directly into level ground. If you want to make a living structure, the weeds must be cleared and the ground kept damp. If you make it from willow, and do not want it to root, you should stand the rods that will go into the ground in a bucket of wood treatment first. In this case it will last only a few years, and you could turn it into "topiary" by planting ornamental ivy at the base to grow up and cover it.

It might look easy to construct a dome but the main obstacle is that all the rods end up in the middle, making it congested. The tension of their pushing up in one place makes a ^ rather than a shape. Included are some ideas for avoiding these problems.

You Will Need

FOR THE UPRIGHTS:

- Seventeen green rods, 10–12ft/3–3.5m long and with a butt diameter of 1¼–1½in/3.25–4cm
- Thirty six similar rods, slightly thinner in diameter, 1in/2.5cm
- Thirty three for the secondary (crossing) uprights, and three for the porch roof

FOR THE WEAVING:

- Strips of bark to total 18ft/5.5m in length, 1½–2in/3–5cm in width, or pliable willow to make the central god's eye. (You could also use strong webbing.)
- Fifteen large rods for the base weave, 7–9ft/2.10–2.70m long, with a butt diameter of about ¾in/2cm
- A bundle of thinner rods, about 40, for weaving the horizontal bands of pairing

- Twenty eight pliable weavers for the ties
- A pruning saw or loppers to cut the rods
- A tape measure
- Strong shears/secateurs
- A sharp heavy knife
- Tape

- A large weight—a large concrete block works well—and a length of strong old rope or baler twine to hold the weight
- Extra old rope or ties—helpful to keep all the rods in place

I **Setting up the vertical rods:** Measure out your space and lay out the rods in the order below. Use a central marker and a stick and string to make a circle. This arbor measures 8ft/2.5m in diameter. Make it a manageable size—it will look bigger than you imagine once it is three-dimensional.

2 Put in the heavy rods first. They must be pushed at least 6in/15cm into the ground and stand upright. Next to them put in the smaller rods. If the ground is hard use a crowbar or a large willow peg which you must knock in first to make a hole. Mark the rods indicated X on diagram 2 with tape. These are the ones that will make the central crossing and they should be the longest and strongest.

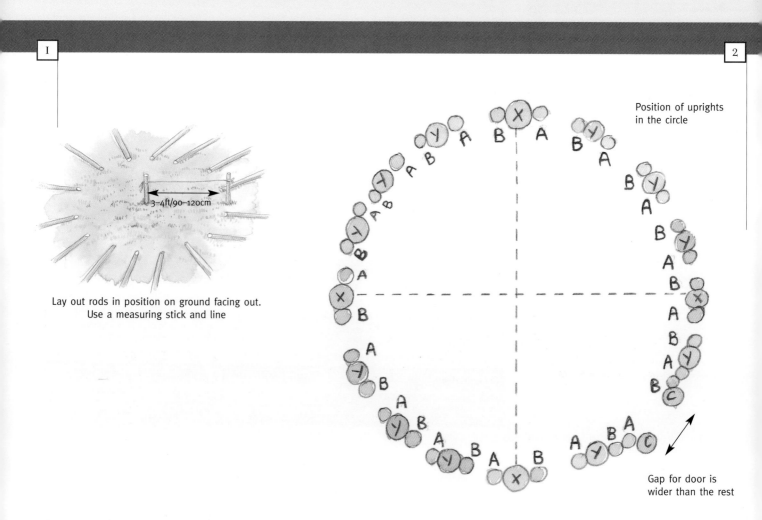

I

Lay out rods in position on ground facing out.
Use a measuring stick and line

3–4ft/90–120cm

2

Position of uprights
in the circle

Gap for door is
wider than the rest

3 **The first band of weaving—the mouth wale:** Once the rods forming the framework are standing upright, work the bottom band of weaving. This is a twisted, ropelike weave known as the mouth wale. It is found in Irish baskets and it will make a strong base, holding all the rods in place. Use one rod for each space, including the gap for the door, 15 in all. Start the weave at the back, opposite the door space.

4 Each rod sits with its butt end on top of the previous ones and goes into the next space to the right.

5 To continue the weave, each successive rod goes under two to start, and then in front of and behind one.

6 The last two rods finish off by threading through by the tip end underneath the first two that you used.

7 Now pick up each end in turn and, working to the left, bring it up and weave each one away to the right one space. Repeat until the rods run out.

8 On top of this, work at least three rows of pairing (see page 24) until you have a good strong layer of weaving.

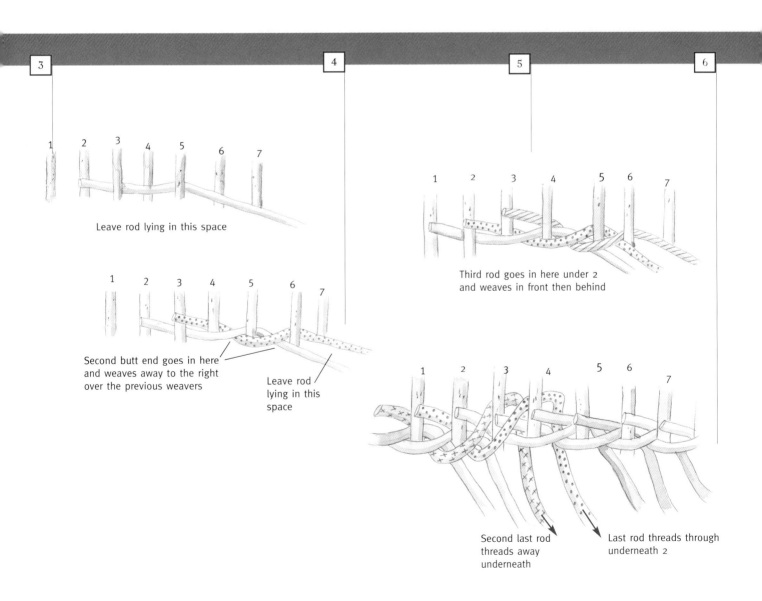

3

1 2 3 4 5 6 7

Leave rod lying in this space

1 2 3 4 5 6 7

Second butt end goes in here and weaves away to the right over the previous weavers

4

Leave rod lying in this space

5

1 2 3 4 5 6 7

Third rod goes in here under 2 and weaves in front then behind

6

1 2 3 4 5 6 7

Second last rod threads away underneath

Last rod threads through underneath 2

9 Shaping the framework: Now carefully bend the four main frame rods marked X in pairs over toward each other and twist them around each other. Make a good shape. Aim to bend the rods firmly to achieve this, so that the top is flat and the "shoulders" are rounded. Once you have a profile you like, tie each rod down to a heavy weight, which must remain on the ground in the exact center of the arbor all the time. (As you weave and add more rods there will be enormous tension on them and they will try to lift and distort the shape. You may have to add more weight.)

10 Making the god's eye at the top: With the soaked bark (or with pliable rods), make a god's eye (see page 42) over the center crossed rods. Do this with the flat decorative face of the weave on the upper side. Stand inside the arbor and make it above your head. (You need to be familiar with this weave to do it. Practice this first if you have never done it before.)

11 The god's eye will leave a space in which to place the remaining upright rods, which effectively become the "ribs" of a giant upside-down frame basket.

12 Forming the porch: Make the doorway of the porch by twisting C and D around each other. Pull them outward so that they stand upright. Scallom on three large rods at the top of the arch to make the roof of the porch (see pages 36 and 37).

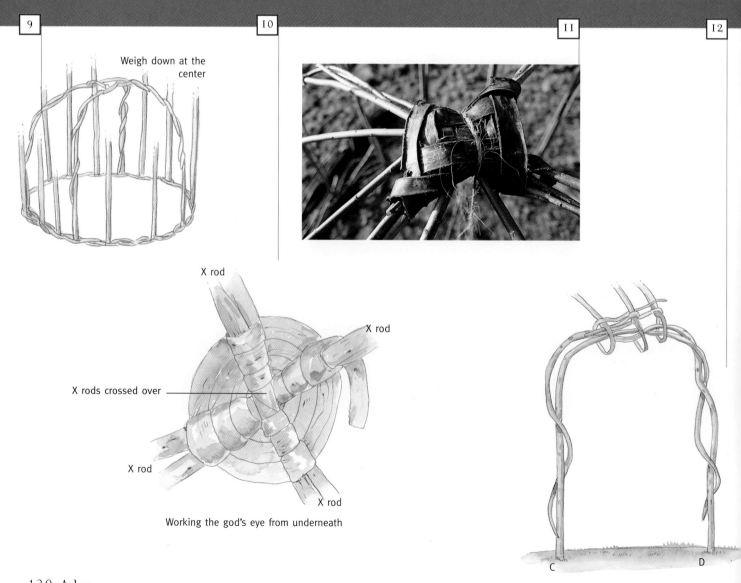

Weigh down at the center

X rod

X rod

X rods crossed over

X rod

X rod

Working the god's eye from underneath

C   D

13 **Completing the dome shape:** Cross each pair of rods marked B over A across the gap in the center, and tape in place against the opposite uprights 4ft/1.2m up.

14 All the Y uprights should now be cut to length and fitted into the pockets under the god's eye wrapping. Use a tape measure to get them all the same length from the ground maintaining the shape you started with. Shave the ends to a point to fit into the space. If the rods will not stay in place, weave a few rows of pairing around them with finer weavers to hold them in. Keep the center neat and not bulky.

15 **Pairing bands:** Above the crossed rods, work a second band of weaving using pairing (see page 24) starting with tips. Start at the center back, use two rods to pair along as far as the porch. (Pair into the gaps, incorporating the crossed rods in the pairing.) Twist the pairing around the porch door rods then work back round the arbor to the other side. Finally pair back to the start at the center back. Join where necessary with butts. Build up three rows in this way.

16 **Second crossing rods and third pairing band:** Immediately above the pairing, make a wrap with a cranked rod (page 40) around each group of A, Y, and B rods.

17 Cross the rods again (A over B this time), in the same gap, and tape them higher up. Weave another band of pairing. This time the weave can complete a circle and pair across the top of the doorway and between the porch roof rods.

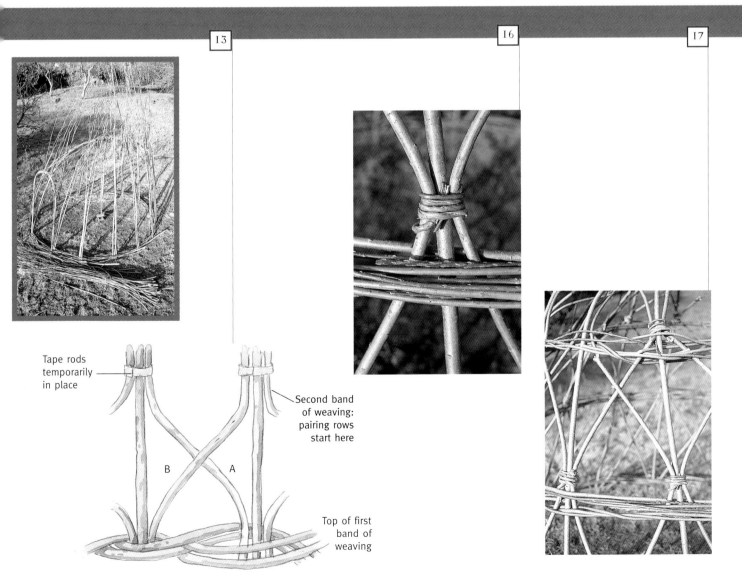

Tape rods temporarily in place

Second band of weaving: pairing rows start here

B   A

Top of first band of weaving

18 **Completing the weaving:** Make a further set of wraps around each group of B, Y, and A rods above the pairing.

19 Finally, make another crossing of the As and Bs. They will be thinning out by now. Work each of them out over and under the framework in a diagonal. They can be cut off without having to weave right into the center and, sitting inside the arbor, you can see the pattern of the thinning rods spiraling inward, creating a tracery against a blue sky.

20 Trim all ends neatly. Leave the weight in place until the willow has "memorized" the shape and will not spring apart.

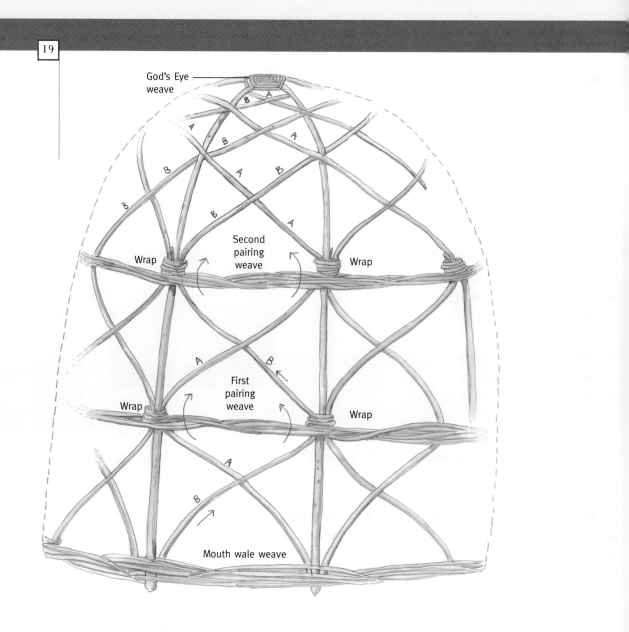

Coracle

This is a version of the two-person Irish Boyne Curragh adapted for one-person. It measures approximately 4ft 6in/137cm x 3ft 6in/107cm x 15in/38cm deep, with no designated bow or stern, it can be adapted to suit. Paddle it the way it handles best. The frame, made of hazel or willow rods, is driven upright into the ground, a gunwale woven around them, and a seat fitted. The uprights are bent over in pairs and tied to form the bottom. The frame is pulled out of the ground and covered with cotton canvas before being waterproofed.

Project by OLIVIA ELTON BARRATT

You Will Need

- Willow or hazel rods for the frame, up to a month old, with side shoots trimmed:
  28 heavy stakes and a few spares, about 1in/2.5cm at the butt, and at least 7ft/2.1m long;
  30–40 thinner rods for weaving, as long as possible
- Pine planking for the seat, 3ft 6in/120cm long, 9in/23cm wide, ¾in/2cm thick
- Exterior-grade plywood for paddle blade, 2ft/60cm long, 6in/15cm wide, ⅜in/9mm thick
- Broom handle for paddle handle 3ft/90cm long at least, diameter 1in/2.5cm
- Heavy cotton canvas, about 7ft/2.1m, at least 75in/90cm width
- Waxed thread, or twine to stitch calico
- Baler twine, sisal or polypropylene, or cord, for tying the frame rods together
- Black waterproof roofing paint, bitumen-based, Black Tar varnish, or similar
- Yacht varnish for the paddle
- Rope or plastic/rubber tubing for the carrying strap

- A sacking or mattress needle
- A sharp knife
- Large sharp scissors
- Shears/secateurs
- A pruning saw
- A saw for cutting pine planking
- A drill and large bit ⅜in/9mm, small bit ³⁄₃₂in/3mm
- 1in/2.5cm chisel
- A hammer
- 1.5in/4cm galvanized nails
- A tape measure or rule
- Sandpaper, coarse and smooth
- Paint brushes, 3in/7.5cm and 1in/2.5cm

- Mineral spirit, for cleaning up
- A pair of gloves for tying down the frame
- A crowbar and mallet if ground is hard

1 **Starting the frame:** This is an outdoor project. It will be easier to make if two people work together, and you should allow two days. Mark and cut the notches in the seat plank as shown, and drill the holes using the $\frac{3}{8}$in/9mm bit. The end holes are for tying the seat in place. The central ones are for the carrying strap.

2 Lay the seat on the ground, with a 4ft 6in/137cm stick centered under it at right angles, to mark out length and width. Drive the stakes into the ground by the butts (thick ends), at least 6in/15cm deep, in the layout shown, to form a rounded rectangle, with 8 on each long side, and 6 at each end. You will need two stakes on each end of the seat, in the angle of the notches, close against the wood, and two stakes at each end of the 4ft 6in/1.4m stick, about 5in/12.5cm apart. The spacing is roughly 5in/12.5cm between stakes, with corner stakes closer together, rounding off the corners.

3 Lift out the seat. With the weaving rods, work one round of pairing (see page 24), starting with butts in the two spaces to the left of the seat position. Add new weavers by the butts as you work to maintain thickness, laying the new butts to the inside resting against a stake, and working the old weavers in with the new ones. When you reach the starting point, finish with the weavers on the outside.

4 Replace the seat, pushing it well down onto the weave. Continue weaving for three more rounds above the seat, adding new weavers when needed for strength. The stakes should lean outward slightly. Finish directly above the seat, threading the weavers through the previous row to the outside.

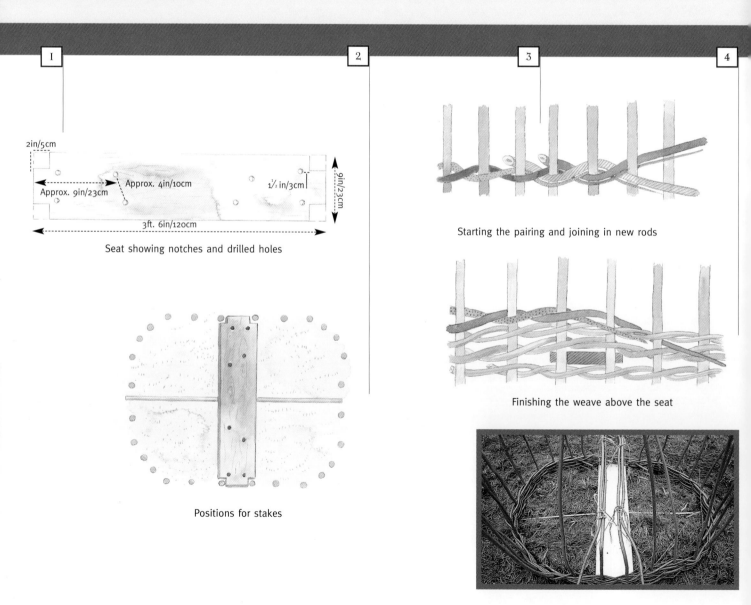

1

2in/5cm
Approx. 4in/10cm
Approx. 9in/23cm
$1\frac{1}{2}$in/3cm
9in/23cm
3ft. 6in/120cm

Seat showing notches and drilled holes

Positions for stakes

2

3

Starting the pairing and joining in new rods

Finishing the weave above the seat

4

5 **Tying down the frame:** Bend the stakes on either side of the seat across to meet each other in pairs at about 14–15in/35.5–38cm above it. Bend them at a rounded right angle, keeping them flat above the seat. Tie the seat pairs together with baler twine on each side just inside the angles, and then tie them securely down to the seat, at the measured depth.

6 Bend across and tie all the pairs of stakes on the long sides, adjusting the level to get good shoulders and a flat top. Keep it level with the seat stakes, with the corner stakes at each end rather lower than this. Ease the stakes carefully over, to avoid kinks or cracks. Look at the frame from every angle to make sure of a good shape. If the material is supple enough, shorten each stake tip, curve it to match its partner, and push the tip down into the weave. If they break, leave them to be trimmed off later.

7 Now bend the central stakes from the short ends over in pairs, laying them tightly to the shape set by the crossways pairs. Tie them to the two pairs of seat stakes. Check the height above the seat, and retie if necessary. (The seat ties should stay in place for several weeks, till the frame has dried out and set.)

8 Tie each pair down onto the two central crossways pairs, making sure that you have a good profile, with shoulders and a flat top. Shorten each rod tip and tuck it down alongside its partner. Now make permanent ties around each intersection of rod pairs— 48 knots in all. A crisscross wrap is good, with the knots resting on the lower pairs, where the canvas covering cannot press on them. Trim off any broken stake tips just outside the knots.

5 6 7 8

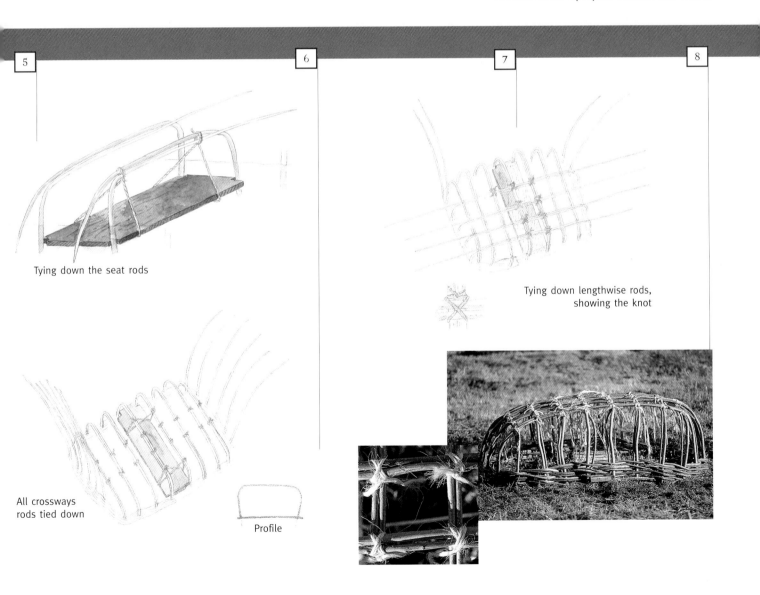

Tying down the seat rods

Tying down lengthwise rods, showing the knot

All crossways rods tied down

Profile

9 **Tying in the seat:** Lever the frame out of the ground and turn it over. If the gunwale gapes away from the seat, tie across very tightly with baler twine around the seat stakes to pull it in. This can be cut away after the seat is tied in (see next step). Trim off all weaver ends smoothly, with butts left long enough to rest inside a stake. With a pruning saw or shears, trim all stakes about ½ in /1.5cm above the weave.

10 Secure the seat on each side with willow rods through each drilled hole. Drive them butt first down into the weave next to a stake, and crank them up from the tips to make them supple (see page 40). Thread them down through the hole, under the weave, up on the outside and around the weave again before threading away. If you find this tricky, use baler twine, taking

several turns through the holes and around the weave. Knot securely. Round off the seat corners if they stick out, to avoid damage to the covering.

11 **Putting on the cover:** Lay the canvas on the ground and place the frame on it. Wrap the canvas up over the gunwale. Using waxed thread, cord, or twine, and a mattress needle, secure it in the centers of all four sides and at the corners, stretching the fabric tight.

12 Turning in the raw edge as you go, oversew it in place around the gunwale. Stretch the canvas tightly over the frame, trimming off the corners to reduce the bulk, and pleating in the corner fullness.

13 **Waterproofing:** Apply a coat of waterproofing, working it well into the canvas, particularly in the folds around the gunwale. When dry, apply a second coat. When the second coat is dry, tip the coracle up to check if any daylight shows through the fabric. Brush on more proofing if necessary.

14 **Carrying strap:** This is attached using the central holes in the seat, and goes around the chest, allowing the coracle to be carried on the back, using the paddle to balance it. It can be a strap, a rope, or baler twine threaded through a piece of tubing. The strap goes down through the two inner holes, up through the two outer holes, and is secured by knots, after you have adjusted the length to fit around the chest and shoulders. If you can enlarge the holes to take the tubing, it makes a firmer strap.

10

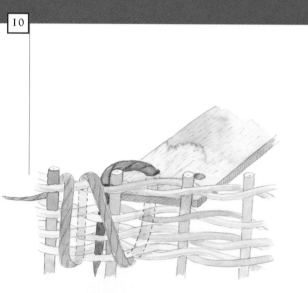

Tying in the seat

12

14

Fitting the carrying strap

15 **The paddle:** This has a long narrow blade of exterior ply, attached to a broom handle or length of dowel, with a T-piece at the top. It measures 56in/1.42m overall. Shape the blade and mark the handle position as shown. Sand it smooth.

16 Cut a 3ft 9in/1.1 m length of broom handle and mark all around at 8in/20cm from one end. Draw a line along the 8in/20cm length on both sides of the broom handle or dowel, at about a third of the diameter. Saw down to this line through the one-third depth, at 1in/2.5cm intervals. Chip away this one-third thickness with a chisel and hammer, from the base end. Round off the tip. Drill holes in the broom handle with the small bit of the drill as shown, and countersink with the large bit. Attach the handle to the blade with the galvanized nails, hammering the nail ends sideways to clinch them, across the grain of the blade.

17 From the spare piece of broom handle cut a 5in/12.5cm length for the T-piece. Round and sand off the ends. Mark the width of the broom handle on the center, saw down to a third of T-piece diameter, and tap out the notch with chisel and hammer. Drill two off-center holes with the fine bit as shown, and countersink with the large bit on top of the handle, for smoothness. Position the T-piece so that it lies in the same plane as the blade. Mark the top of the handle through the T-piece holes, and drill in a very little way to avoid splitting. Nail in place.

18 Varnish the paddle

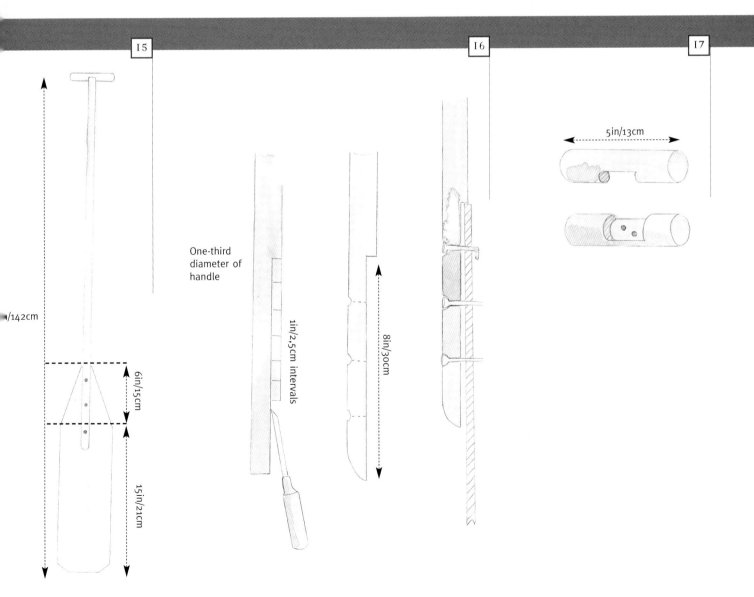

15

/142cm

6in/15cm

15in/21cm

16

One-third diameter of handle

1in/2.5cm intervals

8in/30cm

17

5in/13cm

Enjoying your Coracle

The first thing to remember is: always wear a correctly sized lifejacket. Wear light shoes (not rubber boots), and old clothes, in case you tip up while you are learning to maneuver. Tell someone where you are going. Launching is easiest on a flat shore.

With the coracle sideways to the shore, not quite afloat, step in with your off-shore foot in front of the seat, reaching for the seat with your off-shore hand. The other hand holds the paddle upright on the ground to balance you.

Push off a little with your shore-side foot and the paddle, and then bring both on board before you float away! If not quite launched, try pushing off with the paddle. Sit well centered, with your feet forward and apart, resting on the willow frame. Don't make any sudden moves until you feel well balanced and comfortable. The coracle rocks easily, and will tip if you lean too far over.

Paddle over the bows in a figure-of-eight motion, keeping the ridge of the handle on the blade uppermost and the blade in the water all the time. The blade slopes away from you. With one hand on the T-piece and the other halfway down the handle, knuckles of both hands outward, move the blade in a sideways figure-of-eight in the water in front of you. The blade moves from bottom left to top right, then toward you, and then from bottom right to top left. A little pull toward you before the blade crosses from one side to the other will pull you forward through the water. Paddling needs practice!

Coracle Care

Keep your coracle under some sort of cover if possible. Give it a coat of waterproofing at the beginning of the season if it looks necessary. Avoid damage to the calico from rough or sharp objects.

To patch a hole:
• Cut a piece of fabric big enough to cover the hole or tear.
• Paint the tear quite generously with waterproofing.
• Put the patch in place and paint over it, brushing the waterproofing well in and pushing down the patch onto the damaged place.

ON THE WATER
You need permission to be on any water that is not yours. If it is a local river or stream, find out if you need anyone's permission, like the local landowner or the water company. Always find out if you need a permit to be on the water.

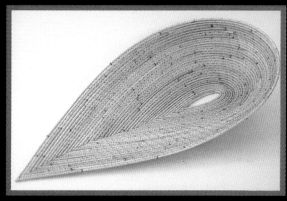

ABOVE: Part of a trio of animal sculptures using willow and frame techniques. *Marianne Seidenfeld.*
RIGHT: Teme coracle. Made from sustainable materials. The main framework is of hazel wands. The center is woven and cowhide forms the outer skin. Each coracle is usually named after its home river. *Peter Faulkner.*

ABOVE: Coiled leaf-shaped dish, made from Poleuti cane sewn with copper wire. *Dail Behennas.*

BELOW: One of a series of spiraling living willow sculptures. *Clare Wilks.*
BELOW LEFT: "Cones." A living willow project. *Jim Buchanan* and *Iris Bertz.*

Screens

Hurdle Screen

Hurdles were traditionally used in Britain as a form of portable, temporary fencing for sheep. Vast numbers were woven, made from hazel often mixed with ash or oak. To make a hazel or wattle hurdle, as they are often known, a wooden plank or brake with ten holes drilled in a curve for a sheep hurdle, or nine for a screen hurdle, is used as a former to support the uprights or "zailes". These were pointed with an axe and placed in the holes in the brake. Long whole hazel rods and then rods split with a billhook are woven in a specific pattern. A "twilley" weave in the center forming a hole facilitates carrying the hurdle.

This ornamental screen is inspired by some of the features of a hurdle, as well as using basketmaking techniques. The sequence of weavers at the lower edge with its tied-in corners prevents the weave from slipping off the stakes. The dimensions of the screen can be altered to meet your needs. The weaves are fairly complex and this project would suit those who have some basketmaking experience.

You Will Need

- Two stakes 1½in/3.5cm diameter at the thick end (if you can, carefully select these to have branching tops and cut them so that the branches fork at 55in/1.4m to provide handles)

- Five stakes 1¼in/3cm diameter 50in/1.3m long (these could be any sturdy straight materials such as hazel, willow, ash)

- Thirteen weavers ½in/1.5cm diameter at butts, at least 8ft/2.4m long (seven for tied-in bottom weave, six for the border)

- A large bundle of weavers, 6–8ft/1.8–2.4m willow, soaked and mellowed, or similar sizes of suitable pliable materials collected in the wild

- Loppers

- Shears/secateurs

- A large screwblock (see page 11) or you can make the screen outside by staking the uprights directly into the ground

1 Begin by measuring 3ft/90cm across your screwblock to mark the outside position of the outer posts. Stick tape along the length of the block against the inside gap to accurately mark where your uprights should be, and change the tape for the next project.

Setting Uprights into the Screwblock:
The ends of the sticks you clamp into the screwblock are round, and will not always be the same size. The outer ones usually have to be heavier. Sticks need to be shaved down on two sides so that they are held firmly in position.

2 Shave the two outside branching stakes to a point and make sure that the ends come down 12in/30cm below the weaving in order for them to hold the hurdle upright when it is staked into the ground later. The other five stakes should be shaved down and evenly positioned between the outside posts.

3 **Tying in the base with the first seven weavers:** Taking the first of the seven long weavers, A, lay it in between stakes 2 and 3, with the butt end to the right, the tip end to the left, so that one-third of the rod is to the left. Lay in the second rod, B, between stakes 3 and 4. It also has its butt end to the right.

4 Lay in the third weaver, C, between stakes 2 and 3, bringing it out at the back between stakes 3 and 4, and then the fourth weaver, D, between stakes 3 and 4. Take it to the back between 4 and 5 and forward again between 5 and 6. Weaver E goes in between stakes 4 and 5 and to the front between 5 and 6. These three weavers have their butt ends to the left, braced close up against the stakes.

5 Return to weaver A, pick up the butt end, and weave to your right between stakes 3 and 4 over all the butt ends. When you reach the right side stake, wrap twice around this, and weave back to your left for two strokes, leaving the end of A behind stake 4. You may have to crank the rod to make a smooth turn around the end stake. Rap down hard with the wooden rapper to compact the weave frequently.

6 Return to B, and bring it up and to the front between stakes 4 and 5. Weave to the right with the butt end in the same way, but make a single wrap at the right side, and weave back to the left for two strokes. Leave the butt end behind stake 3. The weave will look double for a way and it will be built up at the right-hand side.

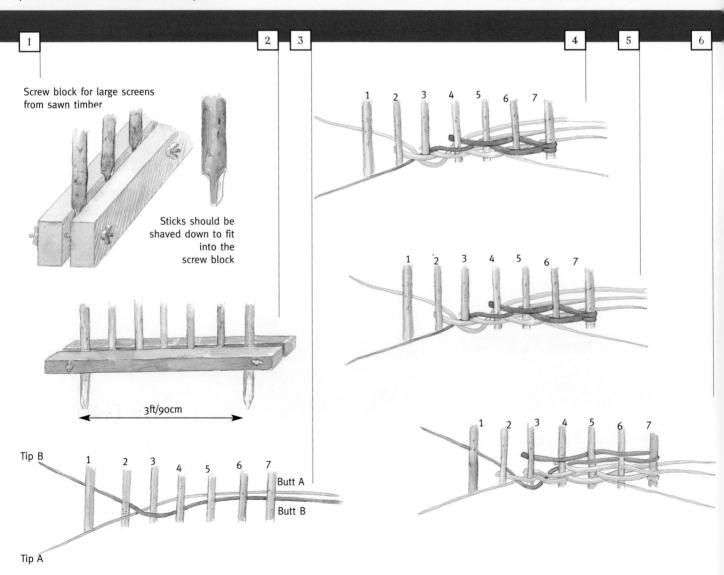

Screw block for large screens from sawn timber

Sticks should be shaved down to fit into the screw block

3ft/90cm

Tip B
Tip A
Butt A
Butt B

132 Hurdle Screen

7 Pick up E and bring it to the front between stakes 6 and 7. Then weave round the end of 7 and back to the left.

8 Add a new weaver F between stakes 4 and 5, and weave to the left twice around the left end stake and back for two or three strokes. Add a seventh weaver, G, between stakes 3 and 4, and weave left, once around the left side stake and back until the weaving is even.

9 **Making the ties:** To make the ties you now have to go back and weave in the remainder of A, B, D, and E. Pick up D, weave to the back between 6 and 7, round the end stake, and back to the left in a plain over-one, under-one weave. Pick up E and do the reverse. Repeat on the left with A and B, using A first. The two diagonal ties hold the bottom weave in place.

10 **Making the body of the screen:** Begin slewing (page 29) using the smaller weavers in your bundle and saving the largest of them for the waling and border. Wrap twice around the outside stakes and, if you join on at these edges, push the butt end of the new rod down into the weave. Weave until the screen measures 19in/48cm up from the block.

11 Now select 10 of the larger weavers in your bundle of 8ft/2.4m rods for the waling. Follow the instructions for a stopped wale followed by a row of "reverse" waling on page 29.

12 Above the waling, weave another section of slewing until you reach 39in/99cm from the bottom.

13 Weave a second band of waling and "reverse" waling.

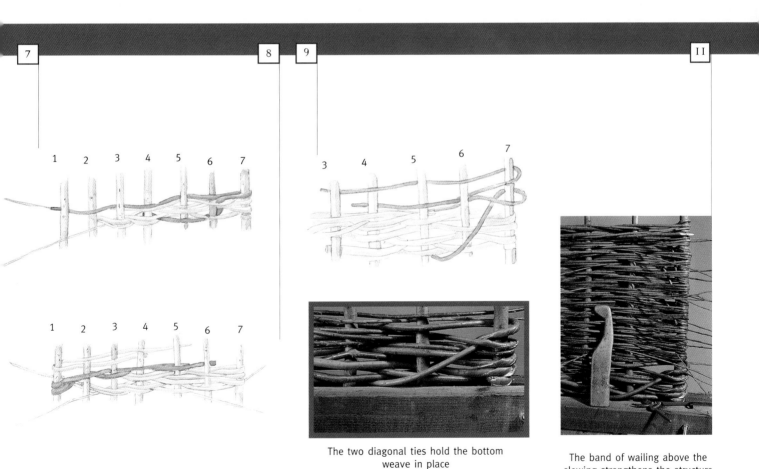

The two diagonal ties hold the bottom weave in place

The band of wailing above the slewing strengthens the structure

14 **The border:** Known as a three-rod border. Except for the branchy side sticks, cutoff the sticks level with the top of the weaving. Select seven pliable rods to weave the border. Slype and push six into the spaces shown. Wrap the seventh(A) around the end post. Kink rod 1 down to the right behind rod 2.

15 Now weave a stroke using rod A, and kink down 2, behind 3, to make a pair with it.

16 Now weave (a), then kink down 3 to make its pair. Then weave rod 1 and kink down rod 4 to make its pair.

17 Use the right-hand rod (2) of the pair to weave, kink down 5 to make a pair with it. There will be one rod (6) left standing.

18 Take rod 3 and bring it up to the inside of the branch-end post. Kink it at this point, cut a slype on the end 3in/7.5cm from the kink and then push it down into the weave next to the end post. The last standing rod kinks to the right and wraps right around the end post. It weaves away from front to back, next to 4.

19 Trim all the ends neatly.

20 **Finishing ties:** In order to hold the border in place you need to make a tie at each end (see page 41). The two rods for this should be slyped on the butt end and inserted next to the border stakes just in from the outside posts. Each rod is cranked and wrapped over the border and into the weaving 3in/7.5cm down. After wrapping around three times the end is woven away into the slewing.

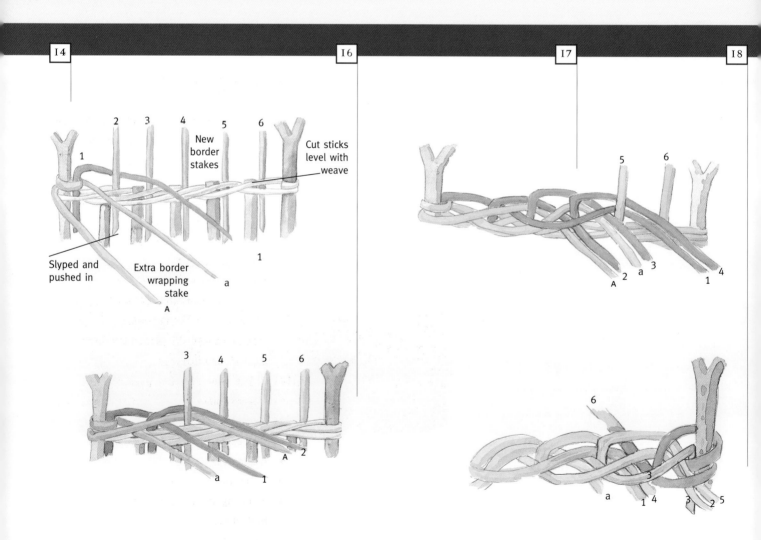

Gothic Screen

This three-panelled screen is a large undertaking and uses a large quantity of willow. You will need patience and skill to get it right. It is essential that the weave is flat so that it will stand upright, and also that the sides remain straight and parallel so that the panels can be hinged together. It looks splendid in white willow, but buff or brown would be equally good, and give it an altogether different appearance.

You Will Need

Thick sticks from two-year-old willow as follows:

- Six ³⁄₄in/2cm diameter at the butt end and at least 6ft/1.8m long (these are the outer sticks of the panels)
- Three stout lengths of 30in/76cm diameter for the bases of the panels
- Fifteen medium-diameter sticks at least 69in/1.75m long
- Thirty six smaller-diameter sticks
- A bolt of 5ft/1.5m white willow
- Part of a bolt of 6ft/1.8m willow (approximately half)—sorted into thick, medium, and thin rods
- A large screwblock (see page 11)
- A sharp knife
- Shears/secateurs
- A rapping iron with a ring at one end
- A spirit level
- A long wooden ruler
- A pruning saw (or loppers) to cut through thick sticks
- A large sheet of paper 25in/63.5cm x 67in/1.7m for a template
- A black marker

Panel A

[1] **To make the template:** Copy the template at the end of the project onto your paper, scaling it up to full size. Soak only enough sticks for one panel at a time and weavers for one session, since the white willow is easy to soak and quick to spoil. It is best to make this screen slowly in stages.

[2] **The first four rows of weaving:** Soak two thick sticks (a), five medium sticks (b), and 12 smaller sticks (c). Straighten them using the ring of a rapping iron, and set them up accurately in the screwblock. Cut a measuring stick and mark the centers of the groups onto it. Keep it on the front of your screwblock and use it every few rows to check that you are keeping an even width and that the sticks remain vertical.

[3] Start to weave with a row of pairing using thick 6ft/1.8m weavers. Then work three rows of randing with 6ft rods. Now rap down the weaving, straighten all the sticks and hold the template up behind your work. Mark lightly where the hinges and waling will come. Do not attempt to pull in the sticks in a curve to match the template at the top. You must keep the sides parallel as far as the top hinge.

[4] Now work the section of randing (see page 22) using 5ft/1.5m rods. Always start with the butt ends overlapping the finishing tips by a few strokes and prick them down beside the uprights into the weave to produce a smooth surface. Every second or third row, work twice round the outside sticks to keep the work level, and rap down firmly and frequently.

[5] When you reach the mark for the beginning of the waling, stop working the randing weave. Using three thick 6ft/1.8m rods work a stopped wale. Follow this with a "reverse wale," using another three similar rods. Follow instructions on page 28.

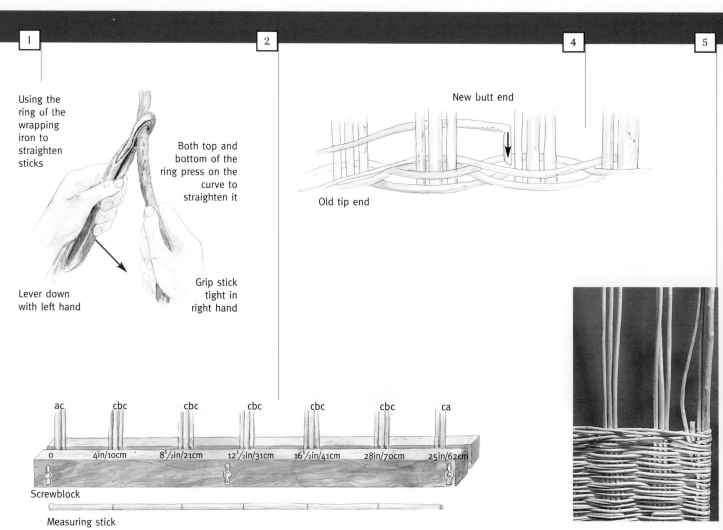

1 — Using the ring of the wrapping iron to straighten sticks

Both top and bottom of the ring press on the curve to straighten it

Lever down with left hand

Grip stick tight in right hand

2 — New butt end

Old tip end

4

5

ac   cbc   cbc   cbc   cbc   cbc   ca

o   4in/10cm   8½in/21cm   12½in/31cm   16½in/41cm   28in/70cm   25in/62cm

Screwblock

Measuring stick

6 Working the hinge spaces: On panel A the hinges are on the right. Insert a liner (one thick, 6ft/1.8m, with a slype cut on the butt end) 3in/7.5cm down, to the left of the outside sticks. Cut a peg from thick willow and rap it between the sticks and the liner to wedge the liner out.

7 Now work the section of three-rod slewing using thin 5ft/1.5cm rods. Begin each new rod at the butt end laying it on top of the existing weavers, following the instructions on page 29. Following your markings for the hinge space wrap the weavers around the liner when you come to it. As soon as you reach the mark for the end of the hinge space, pull the liner back close to the edge stick and weave as normal. If you want the weave to have the decorative effect shown here, always start the butts in spaces 2 and 4 by pushing them down into the weave (the space you drop the tip end of the bottom weaver).

8 Wrap the slewing twice around the end sticks and the hinge liner every other row. To check that you are keeping the edges vertical, hold the wooden ruler against the side edges with the spirit level against the ruler.

9 When you reach the next mark, work a second set of waling and reverse waling as before with 6ft/1.8m rods.

10 Prepare a second hinge liner as before and work the doubled zigzag weave. Insert two thin 6ft/1.8m rods to the left of each space against the sticks and, working from the right, bring them behind the stake on their left to the front (see page 31 for basic instructions). Wrap twice round the sides and hinge liner.

11 Work the top waling rows as before, using a stopped wale and "reverse" wale row. These rows should incorporate the hinge liner. Then cut off the hinge liner flush with the top of the waling

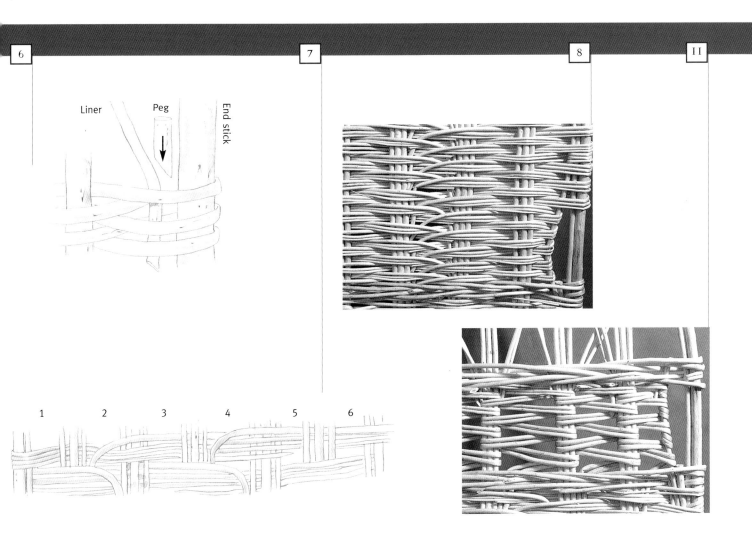

Liner   Peg   End stick

1   2   3   4   5   6

12 **Shaping the outside sticks into an arch:** At this point you can shape the top. Take the panel out of the screwblock and soak the top portion of the screen so that the two outside sticks are pliable. Lay it flat over the template and bend into shape.

13 Cut and shave the top sticks as shown. Tape or pin them temporarily in place and put the panel back in the screwblock while you work the decorative top.

14 Slype and push eight 6ft/1.8m rods into the spaces shown and weave them into place.

15 Twist them over the frame and rope them back on themselves, threading them away into the weaving. Cut the vertical sticks at an angle as shown. Finally thread two extra rods in at X and Y and wrap them up to the top and down to hold in the central sticks. Trim all ends neatly.

> **HINT**
> If you need to stop weaving for a few hours or overnight you should keep the sticks damp by laying the panel flat and covering it with a damp towel.

Panel B

16 This is worked exactly the same, except that hinge spaces are on the left.

Panel C

17 This is worked the same, with hinges on both right and left, up to the top waling. The top is curved round to match the template with both ends of the stick shaved.

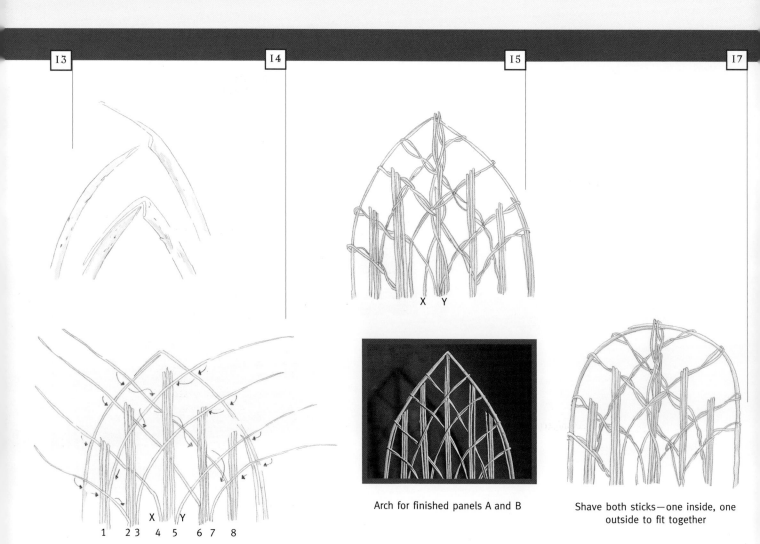

Arch for finished panels A and B

Shave both sticks—one inside, one outside to fit together

Finishing

1 Finish the panels by sawing all the sticks at the bottom flush and level except the outside two of each panel.

2 For each panel cut a length of thick stick 8in/20cm longer than the width of the panel. Saw and shave down the ends to remove the pith. Make them sharply pointed.

3 Soak the stick well and kink the two ends. Then rap it into the weave inside the outside sticks. Trim the outer sticks level.

Joining the panels

4 Put panels A and C into the screwblock making sure the bottoms are level. Hold the end of a 6ft/1.8m rod against the side stick of panel A in the hinge space and crank the rest of the rod. Work the cranked rod in a figure-of-eight hinge for five or six rows. Make sure the tip end threads away down the center.

5 Then add a second rod from the top and crank it in the same way before weaving it in a figure-of-eight. Soap or tallow rubbed on the rod will stop it squeaking. Wrap the second rod in a figure-of-eight down to the first wrap. Thread the tip back up to the left.

6 Once two panels are hinged together the third is easy to attach with all three standing on the ground. The rods making the hinge should not be woven too tightly. The panels should be able to fold forward and backward.

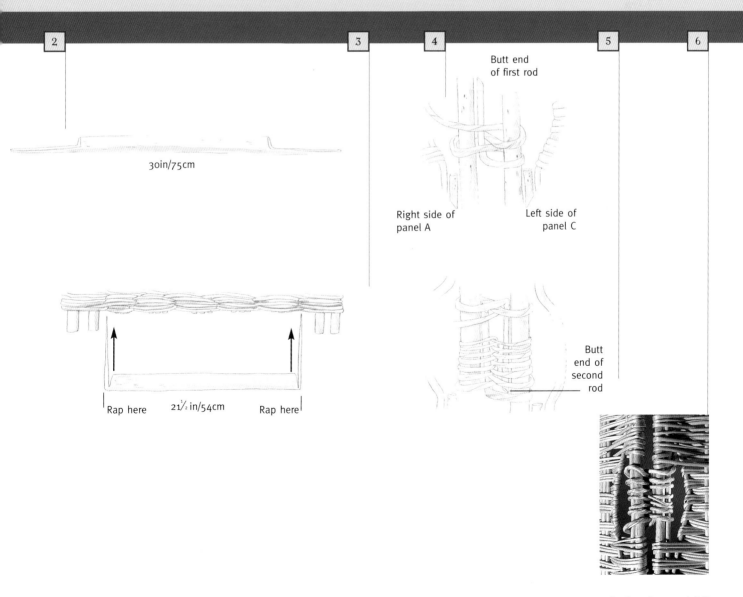

2

30in/75cm

21½in/54cm

Rap here   Rap here

3

4

Butt end of first rod

Right side of panel A

Left side of panel C

5

6

Butt end of second rod

Template for Gothic Screen

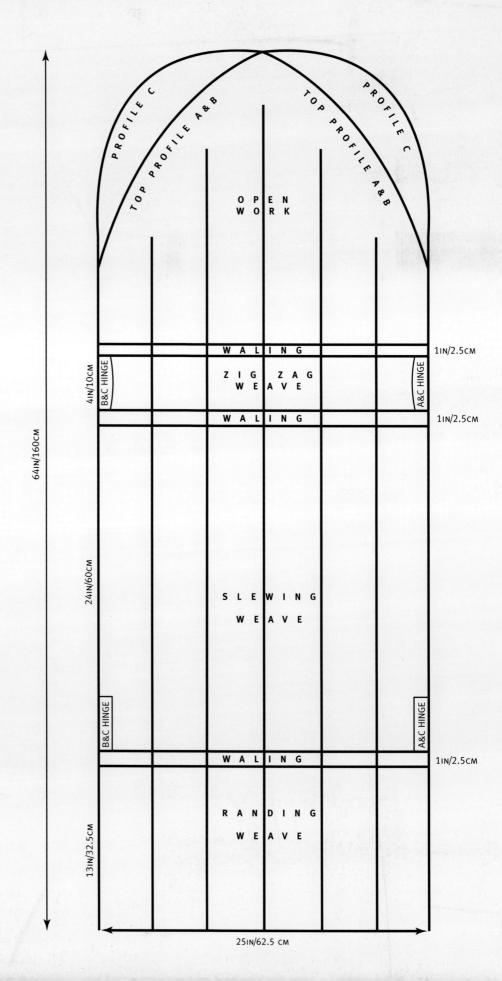

PROFILE C

TOP PROFILE A & B

TOP PROFILE A & B

PROFILE C

OPEN WORK

WALING   1IN/2.5CM

B&C HINGE

ZIG ZAG WEAVE

A&C HINGE

4IN/10CM

WALING   1IN/2.5CM

64IN/160CM

24IN/60CM

SLEWING WEAVE

B&C HINGE

A&C HINGE

WALING   1IN/2.5CM

13IN/32.5CM

RANDING WEAVE

25IN/62.5 CM

Gallery

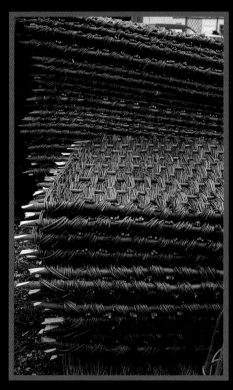

RIGHT: Modern garden hurdles in willow, woven using a slewing technique. *English Hurdle Centre.*
BELOW: A traditional hazel hurdle made from whole and split rods, standing in woodland where it was made. *Mick Jones.*

ABOVE: Boyne coracle, a two-man craft used formally for net fishing on the River Boyne in Ireland. It is constructed with a woven willow gunwale. *Hilary Burns.*
LEFT: Woven conical supports and hurdles from willow at the English Hurdle Centre, Somerset, a prime willow growing area.

Suppliers

UNITED KINGDOM

Andrew Basham, Church Barn, Ridlington, Norfolk NR28 9NR. Tel. (01692) 650998. Screen Willow supplier.

Axminster Power Tools, Chard Street, Axminster, Devon EX13 5DZ. Tel. (01345) 585290. Comprehensive mail-order catalog of specialized tools including draw knives, pruning saws, shears/secateurs.

The Cane Store, 207 Blackstock Road, Highbury Vale, London N5 2LL. Tel. (0171) 354 4210. Cane suppliers.

The Cane Workshop, John Excell, The Gospel Hall, Westport, Langport, Somerset TA10 0BH. Tel. (01460) 281636. Basketmaking and chair seating tools, rush, cane, mail order.

Clinton Devon Estates, Rolle Estate Office, East Budleigh, Budleigh Salterton, Devon EX9 7DP. Tel. (01395) 443881. Biomass willow.

Corn Craft, Monks Eleigh, Ipswich, Suffolk IP7 7AY. Tel. (01449) 740456. Straw.

Edgar Watson, Coppice Green Nursery, Brightlands, Brockley Way, Claverham, Bristol BS19 4PA. Tel. (01934) 838017. Green willow and cuttings.

Everett Batty, Glebe Farm, Norwell, Newark, Nottinghamshire. Tel. (01636) 86464. Willow, dry and green.

Felicity Irons, Keeper's Cottage, Pound Lane, Kimbolton, Cambridgeshire PE18 0HR. Tel. (01234) 771980. English rush supplier.

Jacobs Young & Westbury Ltd, JYW House, Bridge Road, Haywards Heath, West Sussex HR16 1TZ. Tel. (01444) 412411. Cane suppliers, mail order.

Mike Abbott, Greenwood Cottage, Bishops Frome, Worcester WR6 5AS. Tel. (01531) 640005. Green wood chairs, wooden cleaves, elm bark, chairmaking courses.

M. & R. Dyes, Carters, Station Road, Wickham Bishops, Witham, Essex CM8 3JB. Tel. (01621) 891405. Fiber-reactive and other dyes, mail order.

M. R. Abbey, South Wind, The Street, Gooderstone, Kings Lynn, Norfolk PE33 9BS. Tel. (01366) 328711. Rush only.

Peter Montanez, Homefield, Chagford, Devon TQ13 8JU. Tel. (01647) 231330. Rapping irons, wooden rappers, wooden cleaves.

P. H. Coate & Son, Meare Green Court, Stoke St Gregory, Nr Taunton, Somerset TA3 6HY. Tel. (01823) 490249. Willow suppliers.

Sean Hellman, Woodright Designs, The Linhay, Mandin Road, Totnes, Devon TQ9 5EX. Green wood stools.

Smith & Co Ltd, Unit 1, Eastern Road, Aldershot, Hampshire GU12 4TE. Tel. (01483) 539996. Cane suppliers, mail order.

Wolfin Textiles, 64 Great Titchfield Street, London W1P 7AE. Tel. (0171) 636 4949. Calico for coracles.

BELGIUM

Buva De Vos "Salix", Eksaarde Dorp 19, B–9160 Eksaarde, Lokeren. Tel. and Fax. 09/346 80 40. Willow supplies.

UNITED STATES

Caner's Corner, John and Theresa Prentice, 4413 John Street, Niagara Falls, Ontario L2E 1A4. Tel. (905) 374 2632. Books, supplies, courses.

The Caning Shop, 926 Gilmans Street, Berkeley, California 94710. Tel. (510) 527 5010.

Country Workshops, 90 Mill Creek Road, Marshall, North Carolina 28753. Tel. (704) 656 2280. Chairs, bark, courses.

English Basketry Willows and American Willow Growers' Network, Bonnie Gale, 412 County Road #31, Norwich, New York 13815-3149. Tel. and Fax. (607) 336 9031. Basketmaker. Tools, materials supplier, mail order. Importer of English willow.

Mrs Margaret Matheson, 16140 Lobster Valley Road, Alsea, Oregon 97324. Tel. (503) 486 4311. Willow supplier.

The H. H. Perkins Co., 10 South Bradley Road, Woodbridge, Connecticut 06525. Tel. (203) 389 9501. Willow supplier.

Mrs Sandra Whalen, 880 Mone Road, Milford, Michigan 48042. Tel. (810) 685 2459. Willow supplier.

USEFUL ADDRESSES

Association of Michigan Basketmakers (Membership c/o Marianne King), 48201 Virginia, Macomb MI 48044, USA.

The Basketmakers' Association (Hilary Burns, Secretary), King William Cottage, Yalberton Road, Paignton, Devon TQ4 7PE, United Kingdom.

Basketmakers of Victoria, Wendy Stephens, Secretary, PO Box 1067, East Camberwell, Victoria 3126, Australia.

Basketry Network (c/o Melinda Mayhall), 16 Moore Avenue, Toronto MR4 1V3, Canada.

The Coracle Society, Peter Faulkner (Chairman), XIV Watling Street, Leintwardine, Craven Arms, Shropshire, United Kingdom.

Contributors

Fiber Basket Weavers of SA, PO Box 646. North Adelaide, South Australia 5006, Australia.

The following makers accept commissions for their work:

Mike and Tamsin Abbott, Greenwood Cottage, Bishops Frome, Worcester WR6 5AS, United Kingdom. Chairs and green woodworking courses. (Project supplied.)

Olivia Elton Barratt, Millfield Cottage, Little Hadham, Ware, Hertfordshire SG11 2ED, United Kingdom. (Projects and gallery pictures supplied.)

Dail Behennah, 2 Kent Road, Bishopston, Bristol, United Kingdom. (Gallery pictures supplied.)

Jim Buchanan, 3 Greenhead Cottages, Caerlaverock Castle, Dumfries, DG1 4RU, Scotland. (Gallery pictures supplied.)

Lee Dalby, 49 Rockmount Road, Plumstead, London SE18 1LG. United Kingdom. (Picture supplied.)

Jan de Vos, N.W. Loosdrechtsedyk 209, Loosdrecgt 1231 KT. The Netherlands. (Fitched chicken coop.)

Lyn Edwards, 17 Townsend Cottages, Stratton, Bude, Cornwall EX23 9DL, United Kingdom. (Projects supplied.)

Alison Fitzgerald, 18 Bloomhill Road, Annahugh, Loughgall, Co. Armagh BT61 8NZ, N. Ireland. (Gallery pictures supplied.)

Sean Hellman, Woodright Designs, The Linhay, Maudlin Road, Totnes, Devon, TQ9 5eX, United Kingdom. (Greenwood stools supplied.)

Felicity Irons, Struttle End Farm, Oldways Road, Ravensden, Bedford ML44 2RH, United Kingdom. (Materials pictures supplied.)

Gudrun Leitz, Hill Farm, Stanley Hill, Bosbury HR8 1HE, United Kingdom. Green woodworking courses. (Gallery pictures supplied.)

Guy Martin, Crown Studios, Old Crown Cottage, Greenham, Crewkerne, Somerset, TA18 8QE, United Kingdom. (Gallery pictures supplied.)

Molly Rathbone, Sandhill Cottage, Formby Point, Nr. Liverpool L37 2EJ, United Kingdom. (Gallery picture supplied.)

Betty Roach, 20 Iona Street, Black Rock 3193, Victoria, Australia. (Gallery pictures supplied.)

Sally Roadknight, 145 Melbourne Road, Williamstown 3016, Victoria, Australia. (Gallery pictures supplied.)

Marianne Seidenfaden, Dorthealyst, 4440 Morhov, Denmark. (Gallery pictures supplied.)

Hisako Sekijima, 3705 Tsukuda 2-2-10 Chuo-Ku, Tokyo, Japan. (Gallery pictures supplied.)

Eva Seidenfaden, Vissinggaard, Nedenskovvej 4, 8740 Braedstrup, Denmark. (Gallery pictures supplied.)

Andy Southwell, 2 Hillside View, Peasedown St John, Bath, Avon BA2 8ES, United Kingdom. (Project supplied.)

Brigitte Stone, Cane Corner, Staverton, Nr Totnes, Devon TQ9 6AH, United Kingdom. Chair seating. (Gallery pictures supplied.)

Claire Wilks, 76 Grafton Road, London NW5 3ES, United Kingdom. (Picture supplied.)

Bibliography

Abbott, Mike: *Green Woodwork* (G.M.C. Publications, 1989).

Alexander, John D.: *Make a Chair from a Tree* (Taunton, Taunton Press, 1978).

Brotherton, Germaine: *Rush and Leafcraft* (London, Batsford, 1977).

Butcher, Mary: *Willow Work* (Dryad Press, 1988).

Gabriel, Sue, and Goymer, Sally: *The Complete Book of Basketry Techniques* (London, David & Charles, 1991).

Harvey, Virginia: *The Techniques of Basketry* (London, Batsford, 1975).

Sekijima, Hisako: Basketry: *Projects from Baskets to Grass Slippers* (Tokyo, Kodanasha International, 1986).

Wright, Dorothy: *The Complete Book of Baskets and Basketry* (London, David & Charles, 1983).

Index